STOLEN ANGELS

25 stories of hope after pregnancy
or infant loss

STOLEN ANGELS

25 stories of hope after pregnancy
or infant loss

Edited by
SHAREE MOORE

DYNASTY PUBLISHERS, LLC
www.dynastybookpublishers.com

Dynasty Publishers, LLC
P.O. Box 30774
Clarksville, TN 37040

Compiled and edited by Sharee Moore
Copyedited by Monique Dennis
Designed by Sueann Carter
Cover designed by LambCreek Creative Services
Printed by Vaughan Printing, Inc.

Library of Congress Control Number: 2006908195
ISBN-13: 978-0-9789389-0-1
ISBN-10: 0-9789389-0-9

First Printing: October 2006
10 9 8 7 6 5 4 3 2 1

Printed in the United States of America

STOLEN ANGEL

By Robert E. Stephenson

"To the angel I'll never hold ..."
I'll try to find the perfect words
To share my deepest grief
A baby cries, but can't be heard
Death's a heartless thief!
It steals from us those we love
And those we'll never hold
The smiles and dreams life's made of
For pittance; bought and sold!
My soul erupts from sorrowed wells
There is no consolation
For naught, but time this hurt dispels
A memoired reservation!
Lamentations cloud dimmed eyes
As pools of droplets fall
My breathing heavy labored sighs
Death's sting affects us all!
The truest test of life is death
Loved ones gather 'round
When innocence dies without a breath
Only God hears the sound!

17 July 2003

ACKNOWLEDGMENTS

I'd like to acknowledge the team of behind-the-scenes helpers who made this dream a reality. Thanks be to God for instilling vision, perseverance and love, through His Spirit. Thank you to the writers who each poured a bit of themselves into this project; my hubby, Henry Moore Jr., for his wisdom, firm shoulder and unceasing prayers; forever gratitude to Kimberly Carroll, Jane Hutson and David Trogdon who put out a call for writers; Sueann Carter, who dedicated her layout and design expertise pro bono; LambCreek Creative Services for extraordinary cover design, Cindy Cross-Brookshire for gently nudging me forward while providing unbiased feedback; "Woman of Excellence," Monique Dennis, for editing services; Tianja Grant for editing the first draft of my story; Evangelist Beverly Dukes and Carlton L. Gillis, Sr. (dad) for writing poems to accompany this book; Robert E. Stephenson for dreaming up the name for the book and for poetry; my mom, Joy Gillis, for strongly encouraging me to sit and write in spite of the pain; Carmen Wilkes for believing this was possible; Shandria Wilson, for diligent research; Jessica Fogarty for unlimited creative consultations; and special thanks to the following individuals for a detailed review of *Tried and True Strategies for Today, Tomorrow, the First Year and Beyond:*

Cindy Cross-Brookshire
Callie Bundy
Henry Moore, Jr.

Darcie D. Sims, Ph.D., CHT, CT, GMS
Director, American Grief Academy,
Grief Inc.

Thomas Ellis, MA, LMFT
Licensed Marriage and Family Therapist
Executive Director, Center for Grief, Loss & Transition

Fredda Wasserman, MA, MPH, LMFT, CT
Licensed Marriage and Family Therapist
Director, Adult Programs and Medical Education
OUR HOUSE, grief support center

May you each reap what has been sown.

Hugs,
Sharee Moore

FOREWARD

If someone told me five years ago that when I finally made the decision to start a family my journey would be filled with loss and pain, I don't know if I would have believed them. And if I believed them, I'm not really sure if I would have pursued getting pregnant, knowing that I wasn't going to have a baby right away.

Looking back at my four pregnancies and subsequent miscarriages, I realize that one of my greatest needs wasn't finding a reason why the losses occurred but a great need to hear from other women with similar experiences. I wanted to hear in women's own words about their joys and their sorrows in a detail as graphic as they could stand to tell it, in terms as raw as I felt.

Bringing together the voices of women who share their stories is an age-old tradition that is an important part of women's lives. We learn from one another. We feel less alone when we hear someone else say, "I went through the same things you describe." We aren't looking for someone who knows how we feel because, frankly, they can't really know exactly how we feel. But they can know something. And that knowledge connects us; a thread that weaves the tapestry of our lives as women and mothers. Bringing men into the discussion is equally as important to this tapestry.

No matter when loss happens – before, during or after our quest for motherhood, for parenthood – it brings a sorrow so deep that many of us do not know how to grieve. It is in hearing the stories of others that we can touch our own deeply-held emotions and in doing so, hopefully, release them somehow. They will never leave us entirely. We may never be entirely whole or healed. But to be able to add our own voices, our own stories – even if just through reading this book and thinking of our own lives – is an empowering thing.

Telling one's story takes courage. And I applaud the courage of the women and men who give us a glimpse into their lives on such an intimate scale. Each story is different. Each story is unique to the person telling it. But each parent is connected to one another and to each one of us.

Aliza Sherman Risdahl
Author, entrepreneur, and new mother to Noa Grace
www.babyfruit.com

PREFACE

You are not alone. We too, remember significant dates and anniversaries that others may have forgotten. We too, have felt the slaps of careless words across our hearts. We too, have seen our tiny babies tossed into the trash; their names changed to "specimen." We too, have returned home to a nursery offended by our empty arms. We too, have stared greedily at a pregnant woman's stomach, longing for what isn't ours. You are not alone.

We write these experiences in remembrance of our children. For many of us, a phantom kick, a stuffed bear, a couple of pictures or a scar may be the only physical reminders of the lives we loved. Surely, our aching hearts and empty arms will never forget. Thank you for allowing us to share our hurt, our hope and our healing with you. Join us as we remember.

TABLE OF CONTENTS

Part One
A FADING PAIN

Part Two
HOPE

Part Three
HEALING

Part Four
RESOURCES

INTRODUCTION

After my third baby died, I remember the chaplain handing me a packet full of information, including a book. I thought to myself, not another book about grief and tossed it to the side. Those books only told me about the grief process and that it was normal. Stuffed inside, I might even find a story of infant loss about a paragraph long. Psychologists analyzed the science and steps of grief, but I only wanted to know I wasn't alone.

Did anyone out there understand my pain? Could anyone share a similar story of dark depression, of heartache? Could anyone look me in the face as I held my tiny, lifeless baby and say "I have been there?" If not, then I only felt the breeze from their flapping gums!

Finally, here is a book written by moms and dads who actually lost babies! There is no science, just average people and their journey toward healing. You'll read about miscarriage, multiple losses, SIDS, stillbirth, murder, drowning, meningitis, a birth defect and an abortion.

You'll smile with one mom as she reflects on losing her tears, you'll cry with others as they learn their dreams of motherhood have ended too soon. You'll lie on the examining table next to women as the doctor feverishly searches for an absent heartbeat. You'll gasp in horror at the murder of one writer's 15-month-old daughter, and you'll pray for the paramedics as they try to revive a toddler after a drowning accident. Your arms and heart will ache as some lose baby after baby after baby in a drive to become parents. You'll reach for two dads as they share the father's perspective and with each story, you'll leave a little less alone in your pain.

Each parent shares a soul-searing story, but each is also laced with hope for the future. Each writer reveals what they did to find wholeness, break free from depression and learn to smile again. I've also included a more detailed guide at the back of the book called *Tried and True Strategies for Today, Tomorrow, the First Year and Beyond*. This guide offers tried and true tips for how to get through the first day or the first year after your loss. You'll learn what to expect from grief, red flags for more advanced medical care and specific suggestions to encourage healing. Between these covers, you'll read advice that can snatch you from a pit of depression or recapture a forgotten smile.

☙

This is also a revealing book for those who want to understand the devastation infant loss can leave on the bereaved. Have you ever secretly thought it probably hurts more to lose a full term infant than say a baby 12 weeks gestation? If so, you aren't alone. I think losing a baby feels a lot like a plane crash. Regardless of when the baby died, families still must wade through the same wrangled mess.

Imagine you are heading for the destination of your dreams. Maybe that location is Tuscany, Florence or Brazil. As you settle into your seat during the flight, sudden turbulence violently wrenches your lids open. You desperately claw the armrest and try not to peek while the sky falls past your window. There's no escape, the plane is going down.

The impact is the same whether the airplane crashes just after takeoff, during mid flight, or when the Tuscan airport is in plain sight. No one would ever say, "Wow what a devastating crash! Well, on the upside, at least it happened only two hours into the flight!" The same is true for the parent whose baby has died. Regardless of gestation, death has stolen an angel from our wombs, our arms, our lives, but never our hearts.

If you love someone who has lost a baby, you don't want to skip even one of these heartfelt stories. If you are a parent with empty arms, finally here is a guide that speaks to your soul. Let the healing begin!

This book is dedicated to all those
who ever soaked a pillow with tears
because of a child lost.

Part One

A FADING PAIN

Pain, Healing Pain

By Beverly Dukes

Then there's this pain, pain of healing
Pain that never seems to go away
Pain that is always with me
Pain that is with me both night and day
Pain that tells me, yes, it's over
Time has moved on why can't you
You've done everything to hold on
Don't you see there's nothing left to do

Pain is the sign that you're healing
And the loss was deep and raw
The little life was real and precious
Whether carried, felt or saw
Now they are no longer with us
God has chosen a better place
But the fullness of our love
Prepared or expected has left a space

Why me, is the question in anger and hate
What did I do to deserve this?
I never imagined life being so cruel
Defenseless and prey in such a crisis
This piercing pain it hurts so bad
People want you to get over it
You fake a smile and share the time
When really you just want to vomit

The tears that are shed, every night in your bed,
From the pictures in your head causes pain, healing pain
God caused this to be, not to hurt me,
Just so I could see that the pain is the healing from the pain

ALEXZANDER'S VISIT

By Bethzaeli Safier

*"A voice is heard in Ramah, mourning and great
weeping, Rachel weeping for her children and refusing to be
comforted, because her children are no more."*[1]

That last week of the pregnancy was the longest week of my life. With excruciating pains in my lower belly, I paced back and forth around my house to try and start labor. I was so excited to give birth and finally see what this little person inside of me looked like and whether it was a boy or a girl. "Oh don't worry about a second pregnancy it'll be like second nature." That's what other moms told me.

My baby was born at 9:57 a.m. He was a 9 pound 3 ounce boy who was as chunky as he could get, and as beautiful as his brother. I was so happy to finally hear and see my baby. I thanked the Lord with such gratitude.

I cried out, "My baby, my baby, my baby!"

I could not believe that moment had come and gone so quickly. It seemed like time stopped for a few minutes. My stay at the hospital was wonderful. The nurses there were amazing and they walked me through every step of recovery. Those three days at the hospital were also great for bonding with our newborn and just relaxing. My aunt picked me up from the hospital and brought us to our home sweet home.

The little newborn welcome home event was wonderful. Part of our family was there and it was the most beautiful time to share Alexzander with the rest of the family. It was the most meaningful experience to bring our child home to Zach, his brother. They bonded so well. Zach was very happy to have his brother home. You could just see his love in the constant hugs and kisses they shared. Never would I exchange the moment of witnessing the purest form of love through my children. The Lord was definitely in all of this since He is love. This type of feeling lasted throughout the rest of our little one's short life.

Alexzander and I constantly let each other know someway or somehow that we loved each other whether it was through hugging, kissing, oohs and ahs and gentle smiles. I felt as though I was falling in love all over again. My love was so strong then and still is. I will never, ever stop loving him or stop hoping in God for heaven. For it is there where I will meet Alexzander again.

∽

It was a Sunday afternoon on January 15, 2006 after church that I took my children home to feed and change them into warmer outfits because it was nippy outside. I planned to take them to the mall to buy clothes for Alexzander because he was growing out of his 0-3 months sized clothing. He was so big and cuddly. He had spiky hair, big chunky cheeks, a huge belly, thick legs and big sweetly-scented feet. I love him so much. We had a fun evening shopping. As we returned home all was calm. I bathed Zach and left Alexzander sleeping on the bed since he already had been bathed and pampered.

I finally put Zacharia to sleep and by the time I got around to going to bed it was time to feed Alexzander. It was 12 a.m. when I cradled him in my arms and sang to him as he drank all my milk supply. I burped then put him down to sleep at 12:19 a.m. Somewhere between then and 5:30 a.m. something went unexpectedly and terribly wrong. I woke up to feed Alexzander only to find that I would never breastfeed my baby again.

I touched his little belly and tried to feel a heartbeat. I checked to make sure that his peaceful look wasn't that of a dead baby. This moment made me overwhelmed with confusion because I didn't know what happened and why my baby was so pale.

At the time I wished my husband could've been there to help bring Alexzander back to life. Our son was a little cold and without movement. I began to shake him to see if he would respond, but all I saw was blood come out of his nose and mouth. I did not know what was happening! I grabbed a syringe bulb and began to clear his nose and mouth to make way in his passages for me to perform CPR.

I ran next door to my friend and hysterically pleaded with her, "Please, help me!"

I sent a quick plea to the Lord and said, "Please Lord don't take my son away, please God forgive me if I've done anything wrong or offended you in any way, just please don't take my son away."

In my panic I yelled at the top of my lungs, "God, PLEASE!"

All I could do was to try and bring my child back to life so I performed CPR over and over again until a breath of air exhaled out of his body as if to let me know that he was already gone. In the midst of all this chaos, my friend called 911 and as they rushed an ambulance to our home, a paramedic walked me through the CPR procedure over the phone.

I kept screaming, "Oh my God, my baby, my son! Now my husband is going to divorce me and they're going to put me in jail!" I immediately thought I had failed Zander, my husband, Zacharia, and myself as a mother. I pointed fingers all at myself because I thought that maybe if I had awakened a little earlier I could've saved Zander. My disappointment was unbearable.

At the hospital I leaped from one nurse's arm to the other asking if my son was going to be okay. All they could tell me is that they were doing everything possible to care for him. A feeling of faintness wanted to come over me, but I was not giving in. My mouth and throat were cotton-dry and my knees were as useful as a horse's when on its side. I felt helpless. I bowed down on a chair and began pleading to the Lord for His forgiveness for whatever I thought I committed to cause this. I begged and begged for my son's life. The moment came when I had to enter the room where they had him. I ran to the bed and watched the monitor for a heart rate.

I asked the doctor, "Is that a heartbeat? Is it? Is he breathing?"

The doctor held my arms and turned me toward him as he squeezed his lips together as if he didn't want to say what he was about to tell me.

"Ma'am your son had passed on, Ma'am," the doctor said.

"No, no what do you mean? He can't go! But can you revive him with that machine? Did you use those metal shockers to make him jump?" I cried.

"No, Ma'am he's already gone," he replied.

In total disbelief, hysteria and denial I screamed, yelled and kicked, "No, NO, NO, NO, no my son, no, no, please make him come back to me! Please, PLEASE! Jesus give him life, please, please, please, please! Oh my goodness this can't be happening to me," I hollered.

I collapsed on the floor as I screamed and shouted for my son's return. Without the reply I sought, all I could do was yell in terrible anger. They helped me up and walked me to the bed Zander lay on. I trembled as I slowly moved my stiff hand toward the baby. When I touched my son, I was able to break from the deep shock. Tears ran down my face with an uncontrollable force making my whole body tremble. His body was cold and his little hands didn't move to form a tight grip around my finger, his little fingers didn't point up or down anymore; there were no more oohs and ahs in response when I talked to him, no more stinky farts for Mommy to complain about, no more staring at Mommy for minutes at a time and no more life.

All this gave me a partial realization of his inner absence. So deeply saddened, my emotions moved like an emotional roller coaster. I didn't want to comprehend that this was the truth and that Zander was really gone. The staff wrapped part of my son's lifeless body in a white blanket so I could hold him, but this didn't relive my pain. I spent about three hours holding him close to me, but the time had come for them to take Zander away.

～

It was around 9:45 or 10 a.m. when his little body started to bruise. The doctor told me they needed to take Zander because he didn't want me to see his body change. His body was starting to get stiffer and colder than earlier. I remember not wanting to let go of our son. Everyone tried to explain that it was time for them to take him. I just did not want to listen because I couldn't let go of "my baby." I didn't know where he was going to be, what they were going to do to him, and on top of all this; it was the first time I would ever be away from him.

I am very protective when it comes to my children. Trying to bear the thought of no longer feeding, bathing and playing with him was just too unbearable. They took him to the "cooler." I had to let four steel walls baby-sit him. *How cruel*, I thought. This was just the beginning of my acceptance.

My friends and pastor had to almost drag me out of the emergency room because I was holding on to the walls and crying out "No, no, I can't leave my baby, my son, my baby!" This was the hardest thing I have ever been asked to do as a mother. My son's death had come to us like a thief in the night devouring and destroying us. At home I had to face his place of death, the part of my bed were I performed CPR, the clothes he wore last, his changing area, all the blood on the bed that I withdrew from his nose and mouth, and his bassinet and crib. It was awful to not hear my son cry again.

I don't wish this even on my worst enemy. No one deserves this. Friends gathered around me in a mournful state. I had no family nearby since we were stationed at Fort Campbell, KY which was six hours from his family and 1,027 miles from mine. I felt so alone during this process although friends from Brentwood, TN stayed with me until our family members arrived that evening.

Pain and sleeplessness reigned my life for two days until my husband returned from Iraq. His command tried to get him home as soon as possible. My father-in-law and I picked my husband up from the airport. On the way home I explained that I had woken up with our son's lifeless body next to me and that I had tried everything I could to bring him back but it was too late.

He could not believe all this happened to us.

"How could this have happened? I've been so careful to not get hurt while I've been gone so that I could come home to you guys and I can't even be with all of you now," he told me.

Having him there helped me so much to have hope and look to the future. My husband was not able to bond with our child as much as my son and I did. I thought he didn't quite understand my feelings, but later realized that men deal with things differently than women do at times. His experience was different than mine. I remember he was trying to be understanding and so full of care for me. I expressed the same care for him because I knew he was grieving quietly. My husband did help me through some of the grieving process until he returned to Iraq 25 days after it all happened.

The days after he came home were full of visits to mortuary affairs[2] and the funeral home. I had scheduled a meeting at the funeral home to prepare our son for his wake. As we made our way to a solitary, vault-like room we could feel the cold air grip us. We trembled in sadness because we knew we were going dress our son together for the last time. As my husband and I walked over to the table, I broke down in tears when my husband said, "Oh my buddy, he's gotten so big. I can't even recognize him, he's gotten so big."

I picked up our baby and sang him a lullaby in Spanish. We bought him a beautiful christening outfit, socks and shoes. We both cried as we dressed our son and he didn't kick back and forth to pull away from his pants. He just laid there motionless. I tried holding him again, but all I could do was put my face next to his and cry uncontrollably. My husband stood behind me to give me some time with our son. We felt so broken inside.

We finally gathered our things and went home to prepare for "the tomorrow" we both dreaded. At the funeral we had some time alone to ourselves and with friends and family. The funeral was held with reverence for our little guy and almost everyone I knew paid their respects. Afterward our church had a big lunch for the family and friends who helped that time seem not so hard. That feeling didn't last long because we had to prepare for the family funeral which was 6 hours away. Back home our family took care of all the arrangements. Going through everything again - I just couldn't handle it.

I broke down and yelled, "My son, I want my son back! Give me my son back!"

My husband and father held me down until I calmed down. I collapsed on my knees over a chair and cried. I just couldn't bear the pain of knowing we were going to bury him and he would be gone until we met in Heaven. It seemed too long of a wait. The time came for the burial ceremony. We had a small service under a green canopy to commemorate our son's encounter with Jesus. My husband carried the small casket to the area Zander would be buried. We both watched as they lowered our son into the ground and finally covered him up. For some reason, I felt peace and closure in my heart after we buried him. It was a sense of "it's all over." But I was so wrong. What awaited me were sleepless nights, endless hurt, rivers of tears and loneliness.

It's been three months and I have been able to claim some happiness and fulfillment now. I don't feel as empty now that I focus on God - my son's babysitter. I know Alexzander is safe and protected from any pain and disease that his future might have held. For all things occur because the Lord knows our strengths, and weaknesses. Overall, His perfect will must be done.

Bethzaeli Safier is a military wife and loving mother. She stays sane through prayer, singing, drawing, volunteering at church, and in the Family Readiness Group. She resides on Fort Campbell, KY

1 Jeremiah 31: 15 (NIV)
2 The military handles funeral arrangements through the mortuary affairs office.

BORN AN ANGEL

By Sherry Hines

"I can do all things through Christ who strengthens me."[1]

I found out I was pregnant for the third time when I was 21-years-old. I had already miscarried two babies when I was 8 weeks pregnant, and wasn't sure if I would ever have a successful pregnancy. I breathed a sigh of relief after I made it through my first trimester. I assumed there was nothing more to be worried about except for giving birth. Little did I know.

When I was 36 weeks along, I woke up on a Saturday morning and realized I hadn't done my kick counts recently. The week before had been so busy; I didn't even have time to finish the nursery. I decided to do my kick counts in bed so I could put off getting up and starting the day. No matter what I tried I couldn't get the baby to move. Finally I called my husband, Tommy, in to try. When he didn't have any luck, I tried eating something sweet. When that didn't work, I started getting nervous.

As I was calling the doctor I was telling myself it's probably nothing. I wanted to think it was normal, but my gut was whispering to me, telling me it was not okay. You know how that intuition starts warning you, or perhaps preparing you for what is to come. When the doctor advised us to go to the hospital, that whisper grew louder. The drive to the hospital was nerve-racking; every car driving too slow, every red light felt like an eternity. On the long walk to the OB floor, my fears seemed to increase with every step. Once I was inside and on the table, waiting for the ultrasound to begin, my eyes kept being drawn to the dark drab curtains that separated my bed from the patient next to me. I'm not sure why I was so focused on those curtains; they couldn't be uglier if they tried. I guess it was just easier than listening to my gut screaming at me. I kept wondering if I would hear the sweet sound of my baby's heartbeat or be left with cruel silence.

I remember paying close attention to the ultrasound screen, but it wasn't the screen that gave me the answer; it was the technician's eyes. It was written all over his face. I knew, I just knew. It's that feeling down deep in your stomach. It's so strong you can almost hear it out loud. The same one that makes your chest tight and the bottom of your stomach fall. The one you just can't ignore.

The technician told us that he was new so he wanted to get the doctor to finish the ultrasound. He tried to mask it, but it was too late. I looked at Tommy. I could tell he was scared, but he didn't know the harsh reality about to be laid upon our hearts. The doctor came to check and told us the news just like he was giving directions to the store. Deadpan with no emotion.

"There is no heartbeat. The fetus is dead. We can either induce labor or you can wait for nature to take its course."

Tommy looked as though he wanted to kill him. I just wanted it to stop. I don't think you can truly tell another person what you feel at that moment. I am sure it is different for different people, but the core is still the same.

"No!"

Whatever the question the answer is "No!"

The doctor left. I guess for us to make a decision? Soon Tommy left to call family to the hospital.

As I lay there, a quiet voice filtered through the curtain.

"I'm so sorry," the voice said.

This was the moment it became real for me, when I went to the numb place. The place God allows you to go where there are no feelings, good or bad. I think He sends you there to keep you from cracking. From then on I was a robot going through the motions. Doing no more than what I must. Everyone did their best to comfort, I just couldn't be reached. I was still there in body, but my spirit was gone. Tommy was truly alone, because I had left him.

At some point, he took me home. Facing the bassinet and tiny clothes set out for packing was more than I could take. I just walked out the door and wandered down the street, until a neighbor brought me home. Tommy was also in so much pain, but left with the entire burden. I just checked out, and only answered questions when asked. Instead of planning a homecoming we were planning a funeral.

The next day we were back at the hospital to induce my labor. Then 36 hours later, I gave birth to the most precious little boy I had ever seen and we named him Joshua Wayne Hines. I knew then what it meant to truly love, because I knew what it meant to truly lose. What a wonderful, horrible, joyous, heart wrenching feeling. Finally, to know a mother's love, and in the same moment, to know a mother's true sorrow.

I finally got to hold my son who was wrapped in his little yellow and white receiving blanket. While looking down at him, I knew nothing else would ever feel the same. In my mind he wasn't dead. He was an angel asleep in my arms. As I moved him, his little nose started to bleed. A fear like I have never known came over me.

I was so scared I called to the nurse, "Please help, I've hurt him."

She tells me, "He is fine. You didn't hurt him. This happens," she said. She then gives me a tissue to wipe his nose

We took pictures just like any other proud parents. The nurse gave me his homecoming outfit and blanket. I got a birth certificate from the hospital, because the state doesn't issue one. They would give a death certificate. I'm not sure how you can be dead without being alive. It was those things that I turned my anger toward. My son was just as good as everyone else's and I wanted him treated the same. I was very fortunate to have wonderful nurses. They were so kind and caring. I was really worried about what he would wear when he left me. Knowing this, the nurses brought him in another hospital hat, t-shirt, and diaper.

Later, they moved me to the surgery ward. I showed my baby's pictures to all the nurses. As a matter of fact, I showed my pictures to everyone I ran across. It never entered my mind that someone wouldn't want to see them. Tommy was wonderful during all of it, checking with me to make sure I was happy with the choices he made. He handled everything from picking out the casket to making funeral arrangements. The weight of it all rested upon his shoulders; it was a load he carried alone. He had also lost his son, but I was in too much pain to notice. This was a mistake that could have torn our marriage apart. My husband is my best friend and I should have been there for him.

☙

Burying your own children is not natural. It's out of order. You are supposed to bury your parents, but never your children. The funeral was heartbreaking for everyone, such a tiny casket, such a tiny headstone. I didn't handle things well after the funeral. Breathing and eating was as close to living as I came. Everyone understood at first, but life is meant to move on. I just couldn't and I was really angry that other people could pick up their lives and be happy again. Eventually, even family and friends grew weary of me sucking the joy out of every moment they spent around me.

It's not that people stopped caring; it's just human nature. I stopped seeing the color in life; I saw everything in black and white. Every conversation had something to do with Joshua. I couldn't even laugh without feeling guilty. I guess I thought I had to die with him or at least feel like it.

Sorrow and pain hung over me like a dark cloud, and I just seemed to rain on anyone who came near me. I just didn't see how there could ever be sunshine in my life again. Everyone needs to grieve, but it's only healthy and natural to move on. That doesn't mean I forgot or acted like it didn't happen. It just means I had to start a new chapter in the book of my life. Tommy finally told me I had to snap out of it. I was 22-years-old and had given up on life. I knew he was right, but I couldn't do it on my own.

That night I spent a lot of time in prayer. I begged God to take me or give me peace, because I couldn't go on like this anymore. The next morning I woke up and just didn't need to know the answers to all my "why" questions anymore. I just seemed to understand that our life on earth is temporary, and one day I would have an eternity with Joshua. Having him taught me a very important lesson—to enjoy every precious moment God gives you, because tomorrow is never guaranteed.

That is not to say I didn't still hurt, but I was able to start moving on and look toward a future, instead of only the past. I would still have that feeling, you know the one, that feels like a knife in the heart when I would see a new baby, or when I would think of my son. I would get angry when I thought someone didn't appreciate how easy it was for them to have kids, or be grateful they even had children. It took time for me to change my view and to look back and think of the good and not only the heartbreak.

I was 27-years-old before I became pregnant again. I found out I was pregnant on the day I was suppose to mail the paperwork in to start the long adoption process. I was convinced this was a sign that everything would be okay this time. This was my blessing. This was the answer to my prayers. God was finally giving me a new beginning. I tried for so long to get pregnant. My time had finally come.

How wrong I was. By the seventh week, I started to see the all-too-familiar sign of bleeding. I knew no matter what I did, I had lost that baby, too. This time I was angry with God. I wanted to know why He didn't think I deserved a child. Did God trick me? Was He playing games with me, or was He just torturing me? I had done everything right, and He was still doing this to me.

I wasn't mad for long. God is good, and again He gave me peace. I also joined a support group. It really helped knowing other people understood what I was feeling. I am glad I sought help when I did, because before a year had passed I was pregnant, again. My son Corey is now 7-years-old and is the love of my life.

Because of my experiences, I did have a lot of anxiety while I was pregnant and even after Corey was born. There was that little nagging fear that something would happen and I would lose him, too. It was making sure I didn't smother him with my own fears that helped me get past them.

It took a long time to really understand that God had a plan for me.

No matter how much I tried to force my own agenda, He knows what is best for me. We don't always understand the challenges God presents to us. We have to remember He will never give us more than we can bear. I try to use the pain I've experienced in life, to help other people. Sometimes you can only reach someone if you have walked in their shoes.

I may not have control over what happens to me, but I can control my reaction to it. I can make the choice to turn the negatives given to me, into positives. God will give us everything we need to get through our tough times, if only we ask.

When in need, lean on Him.

Before writing her first book, Homefires: War Through the Eyes of a Military Wife, *Sherry Hines has had many adventures (and misadventures) as an Army wife and mother. A survivor of long-term deployments, she's often armed with only a shoe, a butter knife and super glue to hold things together.*

1 Philippians 4:13

AMAZING GRACE

By Jessica Fogarty

"Amazing grace, how sweet the sound, that saved a
wretch like me ..."[1]

After two confirmed miscarriages, I never thought it would be possible for me to carry a baby full-term. It is almost ironic that I sit here to write my story of child loss, yet I hear my newborn daughter cooing and playing on her activity mat. I know now that it was the grace of God that made it happen for me.

My story begins in 2001 when I was 19-years-old. I was working full-time as a clothing retail assistant, was addicted to my work and began to train staff and travel with the company.

It was during this time that I met Brian. He was a fellow co-worker and it wasn't long before we were saying "I love you" and moving in together. Our relationship felt perfect. But suddenly, things went from perfect to absolute destruction and desperation.

It was late-September of 2001 when I discovered I was pregnant. I had been feeling a little under the weather for a couple of weeks and my period was late. I bought a pregnancy test and sat in the bathroom and watched the window on the testing strip. I was so nervous; I almost threw-up just waiting. It only took about 10 seconds for the strip to turn pink and the knots in my stomach only got worse.

I looked at the test and thought, *is this for real? Am I truly seeing what I think I'm seeing and how in the world am I going to be a mother?* My heart raced really fast and I felt nauseous all over again. I was just trying to take it all in and let it register. How was I going to tell Brian?

Would he leave me? What was it going to do to my career? All I could do was cry. I was scared and didn't know how Brian would react to the news.

Before I could share the news, I needed to know how it made *me* feel. All I knew is I had a big ole mess inside my head and I was trying to untangle it one emotion at a time. Since the pregnancy was unplanned, I was more scared than anything. I obviously had no experience and for so long I had been focusing on myself and a career. I knew with a baby, all that would drastically change and my focus would also have to change.

It didn't take long for me to adjust to the idea of being a mom. I thought of the bond my mother and I share and knew I wanted that with my own child someday. That day had finally come and God blessed me with a growing miracle. There wasn't a doubt in my mind that I wanted to raise this child and be a wonderful parent.

When I talked to Brian, I remember him blankly staring into the room, just as I had in the bathroom earlier the same day. It was okay for him to be confused, shocked and even scared. What I didn't expect was for him to say that we couldn't keep the baby. After all the deliberating in silence, that was all he could muster? He didn't want to keep the baby? What on earth was he thinking? I instantly jumped on his case. There was one thing I knew; I would raise our baby on my own, regardless of how he felt.

I moved back home only a couple days later. It felt good to be around my family again, however, breaking the news to them seemed impossible. I was afraid they wouldn't look at my baby as a blessing – but as a mistake I had made. So, because I didn't know what it would do to my family or if it would tear us apart, I kept my pregnancy hidden.

෴

Before I knew it, three months had passed. The pregnancy seemed to be going wonderfully and I was beginning to really get excited about having a child. I felt blessed about being pregnant. Still, my family and co-workers had no idea of the change in my life.

It was a week before Christmas and I was going to spend a few days training staff at a store an hour away. The morning I was supposed to leave, I started to cramp and was spotting lightly. I thought I should play it safe, so I called the doctor to explain what was going on. He told me it was probably my uterus expanding and it wasn't uncommon to have those symptoms in early pregnancy. He said if I developed a fever or if the bleeding got excessively worse, then I needed to immediately go to the emergency room. They reassured me that traveling and being on my feet for long hours would be fine.

The first day of work went rather smoothly. Despite a good night's rest, the next morning I woke up with horrible, sharp cramps. I instantly felt sick to my stomach. I made it to the bathroom, but it took some effort. The bleeding had increased slightly and was a little brighter in color. I was scared, but knew I had to be at the store in less than an hour. The staff depended on me, and I thought my manager would think I was a failure if I called to say I needed to go home because I was sick. I mean, he didn't even know I was pregnant, so I really didn't want to tell him I thought I was having a miscarriage.

At this point, I felt more alone than ever. I was an emotional wreck and had no one to lean on, yell at, cry to, or unload all of the pain I was feeling inside. I had the most excruciating cramps I could imagine. It literally felt like somebody was gutting my insides. I was sick to my stomach and had body aches and chills. At the same time, I was burning up with a fever.

I also felt emotional pain. I knew in my mind what was happening and I couldn't stop it. There was no turning it back; it was real and it was happening. I felt my child dying inside of me. It was so painful because I wanted more than anything to make it stop. I wanted to tell my child that they were going to be fine. I wanted to say they would be okay and we would be a family. But I couldn't stop the miscarriage. Everything I was planning for and hoping for was dying.

When I got to work everyone knew something was terribly wrong because I could barely stand or walk, and I was extremely pale. I told them I felt a little under the weather and that I would be okay. I tried to hide that I was in agonizing pain and my bleeding was now extremely heavy. I went to the bathroom several times to gag and to check my pad for clots. I kept telling myself I just needed to hang in there until the evening. I planned to go to the local hospital as soon as I could.

I didn't make it to the ER on my own that evening. An ambulance had to come to my job and the paramedics picked me up off of the bathroom floor. The pain and bleeding were so bad I knew I needed medical attention. I was gagging non-stop, felt very dizzy and when I had gone to the bathroom, there in the toilet was the life of my baby. I began yelling for one of the girls in the store and asked her to call the ambulance. I lay on the floor and she stayed with me until the paramedics arrived.

When they arrived, I explained to the medics that I was four months pregnant, so they scooped what was left of my child from the toilet. At the emergency room, doctors and nurses examined me. The sample the paramedics retrieved was taken to the lab for testing. After an ultrasound, confirming that I lost my baby, a doctor thoroughly checked to make sure everything was gone and that I wouldn't need a D&C. I remember laying there in the room sobbing uncontrollably and asking God why it happened to me and my child. Why wasn't I good enough? What did I do wrong? Why did He have to take the life of my child? No doctor, no piece of paper and no laboratory test could answer those questions.

I wondered who I was going to call and how would I explain everything to that person. My parents were on vacation, so my brother came to pick me up. He asked me what happened and all I told him was I had a bad period that made me sick. I didn't have the heart or the energy to tell him what really went wrong or what I hid from the family. Hiding had become a routine during the pregnancy, so why should this be any different? I didn't want to look my family in the face and tell them I lost a baby I had been keeping from them, or that I failed at something so important. I wasn't fine and didn't know if I would be fine. I just sat there and cried in the truck, but he didn't push me with questions.

I thought about everything that happened. When I was miscarrying I kept passing large clots of blood and tissue throughout the day and knew without a doubt, that each piece was just a little more of my baby's life. I knew the baby no longer had a beating heart or was moving, but was drifting away. I don't know what is worse; to lose your child at once or to lose your baby a little piece at a time. When the latter happens, you don't know when the bleeding and the pain are going to end. Just like that – everything – was all gone. When that toilet flushed, the life inside me seemed to be sucked right out and I felt absolute emptiness and heartbreak.

∽

For me, miscarriage was a complete, total loss and failure. Even though I had been taking my vitamins, eating right and going to my scheduled doctor appointments, I still managed to lose my child. For the first time in my life, I had no control. I wanted to die. I wanted my baby back so badly and I screamed inside. If anything was hell on earth, this was it for me. I had turned from family, friends and most importantly God. I felt as though my body was on fire with anger and pain and I was completely alone in my sorrow.

I was physically sick and slept for what seemed like days. I hid in my room and didn't talk to anyone. No one could bring back my baby and they couldn't fill the emptiness that consumed me. I cried a lot. The whole experience left me extremely weak physically, emotionally and most of all, spiritually. I was angry with myself, with my job for bringing me so much stress and with Brian for not sticking by my side. Mostly, I was angry with God. I can't deny that I blamed Him for my loss and for depriving me of motherhood. I would spend many times just yelling at Him and throwing my fists as if I were in a real fight with Him. And I was. I was mad and hated the way I felt. I found it hard to even look at myself in the mirror. I wanted to disappear. I wanted to be with my baby.

I went back to work a few days later. No one knew of my loss and I definitely didn't care to share it. For a few years, I kept the secret from my family. I didn't want to tell them about a child that would never be. It just felt pointless at the time.

It wasn't until a second miscarriage, in December of 2004, that I shared my experience with some close friends and my mother. How can you love something you never had? That question came up a lot when I was trying to make heads or tails of my difficulty in carrying a child. And like Brian, the new man in my life didn't stick around either. I was alone and hurt, again. This time, instead of bottling-up all the feelings that go along with child loss, I decided to reach out for understanding and help.

This time, I reached out to God. I was on a personal mission to redeem my spiritual relationship with Him and to heal my shattered heart. For so long, I had been an empty soul with exposed wounds. I wanted to understand why women have to lose their children and I didn't want to be alone anymore. I wanted to understand that the pain and anger and all the emotions that go with losing a child were normal, okay and part of the healing process. They would actually prepare me for the next phase of my life. I wasn't alone. God was with me all along and helped me get through the most difficult time of my life.

I knew I wasn't alone simply because I didn't talk to anyone else but God about my experience. During this struggle, I learned that life isn't in our hands or in our control. God is creator of all and He is the beginning and end of every life. I never truly saw my strengths until I got through this experience. Getting through the miscarriage was the greatest spiritual accomplishment I attained.

As I grieved, I refused to take care of my outer self; I wouldn't eat or take care of my personal appearance because it was how I felt on the inside. Once I started accepting the pain, loss, and that it wasn't my time to be a mom, I began to take care of my inner self. It soon reflected in my outer appearance. All this took countless tears, facing the tragedy in my mind and then handing it over to God on a plate. I asked Him to help me relive the pain and learn how to work through it, not just past it. I didn't want to feel the pain anymore. I didn't want this loss to consume my life. I didn't want it to keep me from living.

So, while I went through this second loss, I held on to my experience from before as a guide to help me through the pain. I wish I could say that it is easier the second time around, but that just isn't so. In fact, it was harder because I thought there was something truly wrong with my body or with the way I was taking care of myself. This time, instead of being angry, I just asked God for some guidance, some understanding of why this was happening. I forced myself to accept that these trials were mine and I had to force through them with faith that one day I would be blessed with a child. Like most things that are extremely complicated, the answers didn't come clearly or easily.

⌀

God answered my prayer when, after marrying the most amazing and faithful husband, I was blessed with a baby girl on January 16, 2006. My trials had brought me to where I am now and I truly believe that if I hadn't gone through those losses, I wouldn't love my daughter as much as I do today. She is a miracle in the purest form.

A child who dies can never be replaced. I still think of my babies all the time and will forever have a place in my heart for them. A piece of me will always wish that they were here and that I could watch them play and grow. I carried a creation, a life inside me, that can't be forgotten or replaced. For me, the feeling of loss is part of my history and will always be there in some way, shape or form. It's the "getting through" and survival of the experience and pain that made me stronger.

Through it all, God's shown me His amazing grace.

Jessica Fogarty is a stay-at-home mom and a U.S. Army pilot's wife from Clarksville, Tennessee. She stays busy managing the household, caring for her newborn daughter, Ally, and is growing a home-based business.

1 Lyrics to Amazing Grace written by John Newton.

LIVING WITH TRAGEDY:
A FATHER'S PERSPECTIVE

By Robert E. Stephenson

*"There's got to be a morning after ... if we can hold on
through the night ... We have a chance to find the sunshine
... let's keep on looking for the light."*[1]

My mind struggled to believe what my ears just heard. I was going to have another baby? Wow! After all, it had been a very long time and I was in my forties! I had made many mistakes raising the other three and God was going to give me another chance at parenthood? Excitement and wonder overwhelmed me as I began to daydream about our futures.

The first few months of pregnancy progressed normally and regular doctor's visits upheld this notion. We began doing usual things expectant parents do. We bought baby clothes, furniture, diapers and even some toys. We did all the things you shouldn't put off until the last minutes before the baby arrives. My wife, Julie, and I also began searching books for the perfect name for our special, though unexpected surprise.

Julie returned from a scheduled doctor visit with pictures taken during her ultrasound. Pictures! I held pictures of a beautiful new life we'd soon be holding in our arms. These are treasured moments of great joy and I know I must have looked like a peacock in a full feathered strut!

I could see external signs of the changes taking place within my wife's body. Her ever tightening abdomen, swelling breasts and slight moodiness were some most obvious to me. Yep, it was really true and we were going to have a baby!

Time passed quickly as we prepared to receive our special blessing. I thought decisions through and then carefully considered them again. Which room would become the baby's? Would we decide to go through the pregnancy without letting them tell us our child's sex? Did it really matter? It didn't to me, though in my private prayers, I asked God for a healthy little girl.

After completing the first trimester without complications, my wife returned to her OB doctor for a follow-up appointment, but this time the news was not good. The ultrasound confirmed what her doctor silently suspected. No heartbeat. Our blessing had somehow passed away.

After her appointment Julie called and relayed the tragic news. I was devastated but had to be strong for her. She needed that no matter what. I tried to be unshakable. A shoulder she could cry her tears upon. I was more attentive than ever and tended to look for good, even when something touched a nerve. I struggled with my own heartache and frustrations, reassuring her brighter days were ahead even though I wasn't sure we'd find them.

I loved my wife for better or for worse in times both good and bad just as I'd sworn, before God, on our wedding day. It was really tough but losing the baby wouldn't change how I felt for my beloved Julie!

A D&C was scheduled quickly so our now lifeless child could be taken and to minimize the risk of infection or other complications. I was there physically and mentally during Julie's struggles but I am still not absolutely sure whether she ever sensed how deeply I was hurting.

Until this day, I have spoken of it only through poetry, which until now, was my one true vent. How can you talk to someone about something like this? Only someone who has lived it could truly understand and offer some sort of consolation. I desperately need to put this behind me somehow, but for the life of me I simply don't know how and it still tears me apart. I hope writing my story helps to remove the deep sadness and guilt harbored inside.

The wound is painfully fresh though it happened nearly three years ago.

Despite hearing over and over again, "time heals all wounds," time does not heal all wounds. It merely covers them with scar tissue which is easily torn away. Even today, when I see someone with a young child, especially a toddler, I am transported, mentally, to what might have been and though I am outwardly happy, my inner self bitterly weeps.

Would he or she have had blue eyes like the elder siblings? Blonde hair? Dimples? Who but God knows? Thoughts once more flood my troubled soul.

I was deeply hurt when my wife threw away the ultrasound pictures as these were the last physical link remaining of our stolen angel. I guess it was good for her, but gut wrenching for me.

I feel, somehow, this loss was my fault. Maybe there was a problem with my spermatozoa? After all, I was 43 and about to become a grandfather for the first time. Maybe it was something with my diet? I am still not sure. Many other questions remain none of which has a simple concrete answer. Here are just a few of them.

What could I have done differently to change the outcome if given the chance to live those moments over again and would God grant us another? Why must I suffer in silence? Is there an escape from the weight of grief? When do I receive consolation? It seems like I'm throwing a pity party but this is tearing me apart and no one knows but me and God.

UN-ORCHESTRATED

God turned out the lights today
A babe we three created
Why chose He to take away
A life thus consecrated?

Tears locked deep within my soul
Along with hugs and kisses
Outwardly I must control
But inwardly just misses!

No answers through exhaustive search
Questions still remain
Listening from my silent perch
A still unsung refrain

The wound still bleeds
Though time has passed
And grief still feeds
Upon this flask!

God turned out the lights today
On life we three created
Why chose He to take away
One not orchestrated?

2 May 2006

Parts of me died, too, and I am forever changed! My outlook on life dimmed and I questioned my self-worth. It is a sentence for which there is no pardon and one for which self-forgiveness is uncertain. I am left with feelings of incompleteness, an unfulfilled path not taken and sojourns repeated in dreams and daydreams. It's like a maze which has no known escape.

Unbeknownst to my wife, this was not the first time I lived this loss. It was 12 years and a previous marriage ago. Like Julie, my ex-wife lost our baby about 12-16 weeks into pregnancy and like Julie, she too, has moved on. She tried to hide losing the baby from me and it nearly cost her life. She almost bled to death after she miscarried.

It was a lose-lose situation for me. I not only lost the child, but nearly lost my former wife, too. I wept openly and bitterly. My ex-wife's mother grieved with me, but now I grieve alone. How did they put this behind so easily when I relive it every day? I don't understand and am still haunted, but there is hope!

Surprisingly, with help, and a firm belief in God, it is possible to get beyond the aches and breaks the devastation has left behind. Know this

- you are not alone. Others care - I know I do. Many men and women have walked these same paths and in their own way will offer assistance. Ask around, you'll see for yourself.

The road has not been easy, but experience has taught me nothing worthwhile ever is. Even through the darkest hours, the hurt, the tears, the questions, and blame I firmly believed God would not place on me more than I can bear, nor will He overburden you! It is my prayer that you have found rays of hope within these written words.

Lastly, to the women reading these words I say this from the heart; even the hardest man suffers, too. Please don't take it as a sign of weakness if he should desire to weep with you. He is grieving the same tragic loss you are and his support network may not be as tightly knit as the one you share with family and friends. I believe helping one another through difficult times is one of our fundamental purposes for being here.

A scripture that has brought much comfort over the years states: "Jabez cried out to the God of Israel, 'Oh that you would bless me and enlarge my territory! Let your hand be with me, and keep me from harm so that I will be free from pain.' And God granted his request,"

The same will be done for us, too, if we just ask.

Robert Stephenson is a father of three and grandfather of two; a middle aged man who works in the power industry. He is both a Navy and Air Force veteran and has been writing poetry for most of his life.

1 Opening lines to the song "The Morning After" written by Al Kasha and Joel Hirschhorn.
2 (1 Chronicles 4:10)

You Can Overcome

By Monisa Bannamon

"I knew the only way I would ever get out of bed again was
if I somehow found a way to release some of the pain ..."[1]

Everyone said, "It's okay to grieve," and "let yourself feel sad" and "cry when you feel like crying." I had no problem expressing my anguish over losing my first child, but I felt like I was caught in a black hole and nothing could reach down that far, to pull me out. Anytime I saw or heard anything remotely related to babies or children I just broke down.

I didn't want to get pregnant when I did. I took a home pregnancy test and it came out negative. I was overjoyed! When my period still refused to show up, I took another home pregnancy test. The results were positive.

I felt very confused and scared. I went alone to the doctor and found out for certain that I was five weeks pregnant. I cried all the way home and kept it a secret for a few more weeks. Once I finally accepted that I had a baby on the way, I started to get excited about being a mommy.

Apprehension set in, when I remembered that my mother's first two pregnancies ended in miscarriages. As a child, my mom took my sister, brother and I to our brothers' gravesite. We would bring flowers and once we even took a picture there. I felt very optimistic that everything would be okay for my baby. Over several normal prenatal visits, overwhelming morning sickness, and even those terrifying ligament stretching pains, I grew very fond of my "little pouch" and the little baby that blessed me with its presence. One day I went to the doctor and heard that speedy little heartbeat and couldn't wipe the smile from my face, or control the urge to giggle and rub my belly. Ten days later, I went to the emergency room because I felt like I had butterflies in my stomach (kind of a nervous, jittery feeling). After about an hour of doctors refusing to make eye contact and many people rushing to prepare me for an extended hospital stay, I was told that my baby died.

I could see the lifeless body on the ultrasound screen and noticed there was no sound or movement. That beautiful heartbeat was silenced. I already suspected something was wrong before that point, but I never expected to hear that. I had already shed some tears, but upon hearing that news - the dam just broke.

I cried in breathless, heaving sobs that physically felt as if my chest was ripped open and my heart was being torn to pieces. I never felt more alone, angry, guilty and powerless in my life. My guilt resulted from me not wanting to be pregnant when I first found out. I just knew that somehow I killed my baby by not wanting him in the first place.

I became very angry at one nurse, in particular, who felt compelled to lose all sense of decency and sensitivity when she exclaimed (while eating a piece of pound cake during my admission process) "Lots of people lose their first one." At that point, my blood boiled at her crassness. She was ordered to leave the room.

My labor had to be induced by pill. I was heavily medicated due to fever, infection and pain. They used "laughing gas" and for the next couple of hours I shifted between inappropriate giggles and incoherent sobs. The doctor delivered my 16 week old baby boy and I saw him for the first time, in the palm of the doctor's hand. He was extremely small. He died because of internal physical development issues, involving his stomach and intestines.

I stayed in the intensive care unit for three days fighting the infection that seized my womb. During those days, I wanted nothing more than to die and rest in peace with my baby. The physical and emotional pain and the fever and nightmarish sleep were too much to bear. I prayed that God would let me die so I could keep my little angel in Heaven, since not on earth.

I returned to work and almost believed I would be able to go on, until my first period came back. I was at work and immediately left for the day and went to bed, where I cried and felt miserable. I was a zombie for several days, depressed and cut off from all feelings except grief. One morning I knew the only way I would ever get out of bed again, was if somehow I found a way to release some of the pain.

○

I called my mom and cried as she tried to encourage me to hold on. I felt as though life and all sense were slipping away from me. I was so depressed and full of anguish. I wanted to lose my mind and all sanity. I felt maybe if I was just crazy, I wouldn't have to deal with the hurt, and try to remain a normal member of society. I didn't want to go back to normal. I wanted my son, or I wanted to die. I grabbed a notebook and a pen and, through body wracking sobs, I wrote a poem to my son. I poured my heart out and the flow of words and tears continued on for several pages. After the tears dried, I felt weary, but somehow a little lighter.

In my hand was a smeared, four page letter to my baby boy, expressing how much his mommy loved, missed, needed and appreciated him. I earnestly believed God opened a window in Heaven and allowed my baby to hear and feel the overwhelming love I had for him. Afterward, I still shed tears at the drop of a dime, especially if anything baby-related was around. I also continued to observe his birth and death day over the years. I even forgave myself for being so selfish in the beginning of the pregnancy. I allowed God to strengthen me. I've tried to encourage many moms over the years, with a testimony of how you can overcome depression and grief.

God has blessed me with three beautiful children now: JeVon, 6 (my little intellectual helper), Jamal, 4 (my affectionate little supporter), and 9-week-old, Jada (my little sunshine).

I only shared the experience of my first loss in this contribution. I did however experience a devastating preterm labor, delivery and death with my second son. I held my 24-week-old baby in my arms and witnessed his last breaths. I still see him in my mind as vividly as I see my three living children every day. I questioned God when I lost him. The anger and hurt I felt, once again, was like torture. My children were all born prematurely, amidst high risk and complicated pregnancies. Until they were born healthy and continued to wake up everyday, I lived in fear of losing them, too.

I have been abundantly blessed to overcome the grief and depression that I faced. Losing someone you love, whether you had them in your life for years, months or weeks, is a very difficult thing to cope with. Grief and anger that goes unreleased and untreated can be overwhelming and breed more problems. Through all the hurt and dismay, you must trust that God has a plan and a purpose for everything. He has prepared a time and a season for all things.

A time to laugh, a time to cry, a time to plant and a time to pluck that which has been planted. Some of us have been blessed to carry beautiful babies for a short period of time, until God has need of them and welcomes His children back home. His ways are not our ways and one thousand years on earth is as one day to God. Looking back, I realize that God prepared me to be the strong, faithful, hard-working and unconditionally loving mother that I am now.

I cherish my children and don't take for granted God's grace for allowing them to bless my life with their presence. I pray that all parents who have suffered such a devastating loss find strength to continue to love, live and trust God.

Monisa Bannamon is a mother of three and an employee of The Henry & Rilla White Foundation. She enjoys writing, singing, reading and spending time with family and friends. This is dedicated to three angels in her life. Her sons Andarius (11/4/1997) & Stephon (7/4/1998), and to Sharee Moore (Jada's godmother).

1 Monisa Bannamon

WHEN TWO ANGELS ENTERED HEAVEN

By Alisvet George

*"Some can only dream of angels, I had the pleasure of
holding two in my arms."[1]*

Where does one begin to tell a story about the day that began the
journey to the greatest moment in my life and ended in a world filled
with darkness and loneliness?

My husband, Dave, and I had been married six years, which was
longer than most people our age. I guess you can say it was my clock that
had begun ticking. At the time, we were stationed at Fort Riley, Kansas,
and I thought it would have taken us up to a year to get pregnant. I guess
my clock was ticking so loud we were pregnant on the first try. After the
shock wore off, happiness and excitement set in.

It was thrilling to know there was this little life growing inside of me.
The next day, my husband came home from work with a two-piece duck
outfit, complete with cap and booties. To see him so excited was the
sweetest thing. This was truly one more blessing to add to our already
perfect life.

The hospital required that I wait until I was 12 weeks pregnant for
my first OB appointment, which was September 12, 2001. The doctor
was concerned about my weight and how big I was measuring. I, on the
other hand, was only concerned about my weight! The idea that I was
starting to be overweight was already weighing heavily on my mind. I
was constantly worried and annoyed that I could not control it. When
I realized there was nothing I could do, I gradually accepted the extra
pounds and started enjoying the pregnancy and the attention that came
with it. I mean who doesn't love to have people go out of their way to do

things just so you don't have to strain yourself? It was great!

Around the middle of September, I visited my mom in Florida. She was convinced I was pregnant with twins. She said I looked too big for the amount of time I was pregnant. I simply shrugged off the remark and enjoyed my vacation. Well, who says mothers don't know best?

Early October, I had my second OB appointment. That day, I went by myself. The doctor was unable to find the baby's heartbeat. My heart sunk. I felt terrified and wanted to cry. She kept finding my heartbeat which was about ready to beat outside my body! Finally, she grew tired of trying and took me to the ultrasound room. Walking to that room seemed like a 10-mile hike. I was scared there would be bad news. The ultrasound tech slathered the gel all over my belly and proceeded to do her thing. I couldn't see the monitor so I only had her facial expression to go by which, let me tell you, was a hard thing to read. I don't think this woman had any facial expressions!

Then suddenly, she looked at me and said, "I see two heads." I wasn't thinking clearly and answered back with, "The baby has two heads! WHAT?" The technician finally shows some kind of facial expression that basically said she wanted to laugh as hard as she could over that comment. Instead of laughing, she replied, "No honey, there are two very jumpy babies in there." *My* facial expression must have still read confusion because she finally told me I was pregnant with twins. I was beyond shocked, beyond stunned. I don't think a word exists for what I was that day. All I thought was Dave missed this appointment and this moment. We met for lunch that afternoon, so I brought the ultrasound picture and showed him at the restaurant. He couldn't make out what was in the picture so; I told him it was two. He asked, "Two what?"

"Babies," I responded.

He looked at me and was just as shocked as I was when I found out. After sharing the news with Dave, I felt something other than speechlessness. I felt excitement. We were going to be the parents of twins! How special and unique was that? The happiness really started to hit and babies were all we could talk about. We bought matching outfits and a baby book all about twins. We even decided to plan a trip to Las Vegas as our last childless vacation. Even though I was 19 weeks pregnant, I was going to enjoy my vacation. I did too.

I took pictures upon pictures in Vegas to show our little babies what we did while they were inside of mommy. After our trip, we had another ultrasound, this time we would find out the sex of the babies. To add to our perfect lives, our twins would be fraternal, one girl and one boy. We started calling them *Amber*crombie and Fitch because we didn't have names picked out. I jumped for joy at the prospect of having one of each sex. I felt so lucky, so blessed, so darn happy about how everything in our lives was going. Not once did I think anything other than good could happen. For a long time, this would be the last time I would feel any kind of happiness, any sort of excitement, any kind of feeling other than numbness.

ↄ

Two weeks after finding out about our baby boy and girl, I started to feel some pain around my pelvis. I wasn't too worried because I thought it was just ligament strain. Just to be sure, I went to labor and delivery to get checked out on November 10. The nurse did register that I was having several small contractions. She attributed them to the possibility of not drinking enough fluids and gave me plenty of water to drink. My cervix was closed and the babies looked fine during an ultrasound. I left the hospital reassured.

That weekend started good. The weather was chilly since Thanksgiving was fast approaching. I was excited because this was my favorite time of year. I couldn't wait to decorate our Christmas tree, bake cookies, and shop for presents. I had a million things to get done. However, the excitement started to grow dim when I noticed some slight spotting. I called labor and delivery and they said because I just had a cervical check, some spotting would be present.

On November 12 I still I had slight spotting. Again, I was told not to be alarmed. By this time, I was 21 weeks pregnant and getting scared. The nurse told me to go on pelvic rest which basically meant sit and not do a thing. So I did. However, November 13 was the day; my happy, perfect little world would be shredded, balled up, and thrown into my own pit of hell.

I started the day with mild back pains. I didn't think anything of it. As the day progressed, my back pain progressed. Finally, I couldn't take it anymore and off to labor and delivery I went. By the time I got there, the pain was so bad, I couldn't stand straight. They did an ultrasound and the babies looked good.

When the OB came to check my cervix, he gave the worst news of my life. I was in full blown labor and Baby A's sac was bulging. We were told our little girl would be lost. My heart and soul at that moment were bulging outside of my body, as well. I felt as if I were in a dream and all I wanted to do was wake up, but couldn't. I had no words, only tears and despair. A few hours later my water broke, and within 10 minutes, at 11:53 p.m., our little Natalee was born. She was born breathing, but because she was only 21 weeks, the doctors couldn't save her. But when they handed me Natalee, somehow, my baby girl turned her head towards my voice and rested it on my chest. There was not a dry eye in that room.

I cried so hard, like I have never cried in my life. I had only a short time to tell her everything I had planned for her. Where would I begin? How would I begin? There were only a few moments to share this immense amount of love most mothers get a lifetime to share with their children. How could I convey to her that though this was our first meeting, I had already loved her for what seemed like a lifetime? She passed away in my arms as I kissed and nuzzled her for as long as I could. Even after she passed I couldn't let go. I knew once I let her go, I'd never see her again. I wouldn't hold her tiny hand or kiss her little toes. How could I let go of someone I just got to know? Finally, I had to let go. My husband was devastated. He put his own feelings of sadness and anger away to help me through this most difficult of times.

Despite our sadness, there seemed to be a bit of hope. Baby B, was still doing good. There was a chance things would get better. As more hours passed, I began to have a bit of hope pop up inside of me for Baby B. I made it through the night without complications. I still cried and mourned Natalee. I had moments of pure anger, moments of sadness, and moments of hopelessness. But I had to be strong for Baby B. I had to think positive; I had to try to believe in something good. But, once again, my life was crumpled and tossed.

All the hope I felt could not shield me from the pain I would once again experience. At 7:15 p.m. on November 14, my water broke and Adam Nathaniel was born. I held him tight and like his sister, he was also breathing. I wondered how do I say hello to someone I love, when I know I'll have to say goodbye? This time, the quiet moments I wanted to share with Nathaniel were taken away from me because of complications with my placenta. While I held him and tried my best to love and speak to him, the pain from the doctor trying to get at my placenta was ripping me in two. They had to give me Demerol for pain, which made me sleepy and lethargic, so my few precious moments with Nathaniel were gone. I missed telling him all we would have done together. How I would've loved him like no other mother could. I was taken away for an emergency D&C because I was rapidly losing blood. After I awoke my first thought was, *God, why couldn't I have died on that operating table?* But I don't suppose God answers those kinds of prayers. I was so angry that my moments with Nathaniel were stolen. I lay in that hospital bed a wreck and in a pool of my own tears. What had happened to my perfect world? What would my life be like now?

Because we lived on a military post and knew we would move often, we had our babies cremated so they could be with us wherever we went.

৹

The next few days and weeks were a blur. My life was in chaos. My world felt ripped apart in millions of pieces that I feared would never be put back together. There were days when my husband would come home from work and find me laying on the floor sobbing. I had no support because there were no groups of the kind in or around Fort Riley. I felt alone and since I already felt dead inside, I just wanted to die.

I felt a sudden anger towards God. I spent so many years of my life believing in him. I had faith; I had all the components of a good

Christian. But where was my God? My God would never let me suffer this way. I felt abandoned by God. I then turned to the only person I felt could help me, my husband. This was, by far, the worst and he became my rock. He was the one who held it together and kept me from going insane with grief. He loved me and nursed me like no one else could. He became the unselfish one and dealt with his own grief alone all the while appearing strong though I knew he wanted to fall apart, too.

I had moments where I didn't want to go outside and deal with the people who knew. I would go to Wal-Mart and run like a cheetah past the baby aisle. The mere mention of others having babies sent me into crying jags. The mere look at someone with twins sent me into an insane state of mind. I had to deal with the thoughtless things people say in an attempt to be sympathetic. For instance, there were comments like "You are young, you can still have more kids;" "God knew they'd be sick, so he took them;" and "Maybe you were just meant to have one child instead of twins." It was hard to not want to yell at them, but inside I knew they were trying to be helpful. I thought I would never have days of happiness, of bliss and of joy. I was convinced this grief would follow me the rest of my life. The thought of never being able to have kids frightened me. I just wanted to turn back time and go to that perfect place I once knew.

Little by little, on my own, and with the help of my husband and a God I *thought* abandoned me, I started to see life again. I realized this had nothing to do with God. God was with me the entire time. God doesn't always stop a bad thing from happening, but He will help us through our trials. I was able to smile without feeling guilty. I was able to step outside and not constantly fear that people would look at me with a sad expression on their faces. I was able to try to enjoy my life though it would never be like it was in the beginning. I had my setbacks. I had my bad days, but there were more good days I could enjoy. I had to fall into that pit of hell, swim in it for awhile and then climb out slowly. I had to grieve and mourn before I could start to live again. I had to let go and believe God would carry me the rest of the way. I finally realized I would never know the answer to the question WHY.

There never was a clear answer about why I lost my babies. It's been said it was Group B Strep, perhaps Chorioamnionitis or simply a weak cervix. I have to live with the not knowing and be content with those few precious months I had with my babies inside of me. I know I loved and cared for them and I miss them everyday. I would've been the best mommy.

Today, almost four years later, I can look at their pictures and feel that love though the tears still come. I can celebrate their birthdays and not want to sleep the days away. I can look at others with twins and fondly remember the two beautiful ones I held in my arms. I have been able to go on and have a beautiful son, Eli, and am pregnant with a little girl, Mia. I speak of our first born babies to my son often and always remember them and include them in all we do.

Life has been tough for us, but our lives are starting to look good again. It can never be the perfect world we once knew. Perfect will be when we reach Heaven and finally, our family will be complete.

Alisvet George is a stay-at-home mom to a 3-year-old son, a newborn daughter and two dogs. She has been married 11 years and spent seven of those as a military wife. She is an avid scrapbooker and stamper. She also stays busy doing Jazzercise.

1 Author Unknown

I HAVE BEEN THERE

By Robin Lynn Graham

"They will be like a well watered garden, and they will sorrow no more. ... I will turn their mourning into gladness; I will give them comfort and joy instead of sorrow."[1]

There are some things that a heart cannot forget. It's been more than 13 years, and I can still remember every detail about the day I got the news my baby had died. I remember what the ultrasound room looked like and what I wore that day. The smells, sights and sounds. The image of the little peanut on the ultrasound screen. They are all imprinted in my mind like a bleak winter scene etched into a cold black piece of glass. There are some things that a heart cannot forget.

It was a cold day in October, and I was scheduled to have a routine ultrasound at the hospital. I was about 16 weeks along in my third pregnancy, and the doctor had yet to hear a heartbeat. I was assured it was nothing to worry about; this sometimes happens especially after multiple births. Besides, I had put on quite a bit of weight which might be hindering things.

I walked into the clinic, finishing up the gallon of water they made me drink before the ultrasound, and then I sat and waited my turn. It didn't take long before I was called back and asked to put on a lovely gown and lie on a freezing metal table. Two minutes into the ultrasound, I knew something was wrong.

The technician became really quiet and soon left the room without an explanation. A different technician came in a moment later, all smiles and friendly, to begin the ultrasound again. After her first attempt, she

41

asked me, in a calm reassuring voice, to go to the bathroom and drink a few more glasses of water. When I asked if there was anything wrong she said that she just wanted to make sure they were getting a clear picture of the baby.

I did as she asked, but was she nuts? Drink more water? After two babies, my bladder wasn't that strong to begin with and yikes! It hurt when they pressed on my tummy like that! When I came out of the bathroom, there was an official looking, doctor-type person at the ultrasound machine.

"Okay, Mrs. Graham, let's see what we've got going on here," he said, as he began the process yet one more time.

This man had the bedside manner of a steam roller.

Right away he said, "Okay, we've got a problem." He turned the screen so that I could finally see what they had been seeing. My baby was just a tiny peanut of a thing on the screen. I was used to having ultrasounds later in pregnancy when there are clearly defined fingers and toes. There was none of that, and the worst part, the doctor so bluntly pointed out, was that there was no heartbeat. He showed me the small black spot on the screen that was my baby's heart. I stared numbly at that spot as the doctor explained that my baby had died.

They didn't know the cause or why my body had not done its job getting rid of the fetus. Yes, he actually said those words. He said my OB doctor would probably give my body a few weeks to dispel the dead fetus, and if this did not happened naturally, then they would have to do a D&C.

I dressed in a continued state of numbness that slowly turned to anger. He was talking about my baby like it was garbage that my body needed to get rid of! It was so unreal to me. No one could talk about a baby like that, could they? When I left the room, someone handed me a paper and told me I would be getting a call in a few days with my next appointment, and that was it. I walked like a zombie out to my van where I sat for who knows how long. I don't know if I even cried. I just remember sitting there for the longest time before I remembered my two girls at the baby-sitter's. I needed to get home to my kids and hold them tight until my husband came home from work. I needed him to hold *me* tight and let me know everything was going to be alright.

The next few weeks flew by in a blur of tears and confusion. I didn't talk about what was happening to me because it still didn't seem real. I told my parents and one or two of our closest friends, but that is all. It wasn't until the day before the D&C that we decided to tell our Sunday school class and ask for prayer. After the prayer time our teacher began her lesson, and I really cannot tell you what the point of that lesson was, I just remember these words:

"I cannot even look at Robin this morning. There she sits with a dead baby inside her womb and she has asked us for prayer. She doesn't need prayer. When people like this ask us for prayer, what they are really wanting is one of two things: answers or someone to feel sorry for them."

I didn't hear another word of that lesson. I was mad. I was furious! I wouldn't have been surprised if the fire alarm went off. I was that HOT! Did this woman actually think that when I finally chose to open up my wounded heart for a second to share with them it was because I wanted someone to feel sorry for me? Unbelievable!

My teenagers will respond in the same angry way and my response to them is, "Me thinks thou doest protest too loudly." I know when they respond in anger that I must be getting close to the heart of the matter. The situation with the teacher reminds me of that and now that I'm so far away from the pain of her statement, I can look back and honestly say she was right. I don't know the meaning she had behind those words, but she was right. I don't know how I can, in good conscience, sit here as a Christian and tell you that I didn't really want prayer. Maybe it was just that I didn't want to hear the typical prayer that is given almost robotically on these occasions. I didn't want the doctors to be granted wisdom. I didn't need my body healed. I wasn't ready to use this situation to reach out to others with Christ's love. My baby was dead inside my "safe place," and I wanted to know why and I wanted someone, not to feel sorry for me, but to at least be able to empathize. To be able to say, "I have been there."

The problem was that I was looking to the world for answers and sympathy and not choosing prayer, the only avenue that would've taken me to the One who had all the answers and who had "been there, done that." The doctors did need wisdom, my body did need healing, and I needed answers. Unfortunately, instead of asking God, I stayed away from Him and assumed that He just chose to take my baby away because He wanted to. God doesn't need a reason, He doesn't need to explain Himself, but I still needed to know why.

☙

The day of the D&C was awful. My husband was there, but when he found out that a D&C is like having an abortion, he was livid. He really couldn't believe I was having an abortion. The nurses tried to explain it to him better, but in his mind I was having an abortion, and even today he says that was the toughest thing for him to deal with. The pain of the procedure was intense. They gave me something that put me out for awhile. When I woke up, the first thing I remember is a nurse in my face saying, "Robin, wake up honey, it's all over. Every thing is all done." And I cried. I laid there and cried until I could cry no more.

A few days later, I was back to see the doctor for the follow-up visit. It went pretty well until I was left alone in the room with my chart. I flipped through looking for a report to see if it identified the sex of my baby. We never knew if it was a boy or a girl, and I wanted to know. I found the report and it was then I realized my husband was right. The report was a listing of all my baby's parts that were found after the procedure. I really didn't understand the report until I read, "male fetus approximately 12 weeks gestation." I ran to the bathroom and threw up.

When I got home, I took out pen and paper and wrote this poem:

The little peanut on the screen
Is a picture of my baby
And I lay there knowing
Knowing somehow my baby wasn't safe

He wasn't safe and warm
In my secret place
Someone, something
Hurt my little baby
Someone, something
Had taken my baby's life
And left the baby inside of me
There he was
On the screen
And I lay there staring
Waiting for him to move
Waiting for him to say
He was safe
I lay there waiting, knowing
Someone, something
Had come and taken my baby's life
I lay there crying
Oh, baby
Precious baby
I'm so sorry
I couldn't keep you safe
I'm sorry I'll never hold you
I'll never know you or
Your smile
Your dear precious smile
It's all Jesus' now
And maybe he just didn't
Want to share it
I'm sorry for so many things
They took you out of my womb
And took you far away
I don't know you or who you are
But I'm so sorry.
I'm sorry I didn't keep you safe.

Writing my feelings in this way was a good beginning of the healing process for me, but I still had to face people's comments. People have been the biggest roadblock to healing in my life in different areas, and this was no exception. The rude and unnecessary comments, the well-meaning comments that are hurtful nonetheless, and the questions, all added together to prolong the pain of the wound. People made statements like: "God knows best," "You should be thankful for the two healthy, beautiful children you already have," "You're not going to have anymore kids, are you?" And when you think it can't get worse than that, a friend comes along that you haven't seen in a month and asks, "When's the baby due?"

There was one person, during this time, who did something I will never forget. My sister-in-law came over during my healing time. I was still in bed with my feet up, and she came into my room and didn't say a word. She gave me a hug and let me put my head on her shoulder and cry. Although she had experienced miscarriages herself, there were no words of comfort, no spiritual anecdotes, nothing. She just let me cry - because she had been there.

I wish I would've known then what it took me years to learn and do. God had been waiting silently, no words of wisdom, no answers or explanations, but He was there. He just wanted me to crawl up into His lap, lay my head on His shoulder and cry. And cry and cry and cry until wailing turned to sobbing, and my heart could quiet down enough to hear Him say what Mark Schultz has so eloquently put to music:

I have been there.
I know what pain is all about.
Yes, I have been there and I'm standing with you now.
I have been there.
I came to build a bridge so that this road could lead you home.
Yes, I have been there.

❧

March of the next year I was pregnant again, and scared. Would I lose this baby, too? Nine months later, a 10 pound baby boy joined the

Graham family and brought happiness and healing to my hurting heart. Did this new baby take the place of our dear Matthew Eli? Certainly not! In fact, when we were picking out charms for a Mother's Day necklace for me, my kids all voted that I add a little boy charm with Matthew's birthstone on it. They have not forgotten him either. We have chosen to keep the place where he lives in our memories, clear of the weeds of bitterness and resentment. As a result, that place has grown and matured into a lovely garden where we can go, reflect and yes, shed a few tears. But when we leave, we go with peace instead of pain in our hearts. It is what God wants from me. He longs to take my hurts and turn them into something greater.

I won't say rejoicing. I don't think I can ever rejoice in my loss, but I can choose to see God and the good in the situation. More importantly, I can use my empty arms to reach out to those who are hurting, and if nothing else, I am able to say, "I have been there."

Robin Graham is a military wife and a mother of three. She currently lives at Fort Campbell where her husband serves as an Army chaplain. She enjoys genealogy, scrapbooking, writing and spending time with the neighborhood teenagers. Robin is active in her husband's unit, Chaplain's Wives Group and the chapel.

1 Jeremiah 31:12-13 (NIV)

7 IS FINALITY

By Christine M. Alexander

"You are the salt of the earth ..."[1]

All I know is that one moment I was going in for a routine appointment during the middle of my second trimester and in the next instant we can't find the heartbeat on the ultrasound machine. I just felt the baby kicking two days earlier and decided that he or she was just resting and growing. My worst fear was coming true. I felt such emptiness in the moment when we could not see any heartbeat or movement whatsoever. I immediately knew the baby was gone.

As the doctor tried to awaken the baby I knew I would have to say goodbye - again. My husband looked at me and before the doctor could get the words out, we both were in tears. I felt numb from head to toe. I grew even more distraught when the hospital staff wanted me to stay the night so that first thing in the morning, I could have an amniocentesis to determine why the baby died, and also have labor induced.

I thought to myself, *I actually have to deliver this baby? What kind of world is this where a mother has to go through the labor pain and deliver a baby that is dead? Why couldn't God just make it all disappear?* I felt so alone; my husband could not deal with the pain so he stayed away from the hospital. I went through the whole experience alone. In the morning, the doctor wheeled me up to labor and delivery where other happy mothers were delivering their babies and joy was in the air; I felt so sick and empty.

I wanted to die as I lay alone in the room going through labor pains all throughout the day. I knew somehow this was my fault. What did I do that had been so wrong? I kept asking God to help me understand how He could do this to me.

◦

Since we've been married, this was our seventh loss in six years; all of them up to this point were early miscarriages in the first trimester. I was well into my second trimester with Jacob. The doctor pleaded with me to take medication for the labor pain, or get an epidural but I could not. I needed to feel every sensation and every moment. It was, after all, my punishment. How could God do this to me?

When I delivered the baby close to 10 p.m., I just held him and cried and didn't know what to do. I knew I had to let him go, but I couldn't. The doctor took our baby away and I called my husband to come and take me home, my anger with him for leaving me to do this alone was overshadowed by the pain of my loss. For the week leading up to the funeral, I could not eat, sleep and did not want to live. On the day of the funeral, we went to the funeral home to follow the hearse and view the baby one last time. I thought I was going to pass out from the pain. When I looked at the baby, he didn't look the same because the preservation process made him shrivel up and look much smaller than he was after his birth.

I didn't recognize my baby and it just destroyed me. I walked my son from the hearse to the burial site in his little coffin and felt like I had no choice but to let him go, physically. But never emotionally.

◦

My first pregnancy produced a daughter who was 4-years-old at the time, and I felt that she could find a better mother, my husband could find a better wife and so I wanted God to take my life. I prayed for it every night. I wanted the power to take my own life, but couldn't find that strength anywhere. After the funeral I still felt empty and everyone reminded me that I should be grateful for the one child I had and some women couldn't even have one. This was the last thing I wanted to hear because how could they understand my emptiness? My love for my living child was the same as the love for my child that went to Heaven. I had to deal with this loss so suddenly and just couldn't do it. I decided to get into my Bible and let God explain why this was happening to me.

I became more involved with church activities and the women's group. I found support and guidance there; for which I will always be grateful. When I was going through this, and the operative word being "through," I never thought I could come out whole or even partially whole. Every minute seemed like an hour and every day felt like an eternity; I wondered when it would all stop? My only comfort came from the One I was questioning - God. I don't know how or why, but He was still with me even though I tried to push him away. For a long time, I wore a mask because I did not want people talking to me about our son, Jacob, and I did not want to express my feelings to anyone. I even tried to encourage other women, although I was still so discouraged myself. Over the next few months, God started to explain what He wanted from me and it was not what I wanted to hear. I was just going through the motions with everyone around me.

I now know that I have grown spiritually and it was a season of rebirth for my spiritual self. God was working with me in a major way and I took comfort in the fact that God was enlightening me to become a disciple and a leader for women through my own perseverance.

Everyone around me said I should not try to have any more children and that "seven" was a number of finality. They said it was a direct sign from God that my husband and I already had the one child God intended for us. I, however, saw it differently and no one could tell me otherwise. My doctor said that we should not try anymore because it could do serious damage to my body and there was a reason for the seven losses. God told me different.

Against our family and friends' wishes, Christopher and I got pregnant again. I was very afraid and my parents on both sides were scared for us, too. For the first time in a while I was able to fight off the devil for making me believe I was unable to conceive a healthy child. I told everyone who said we should not have babies because it would result in a miscarriage, my thoughts about their "prophesy." I said they were right to say that seven was a number of finality and Jacob would be my last loss. I was right; Jacob was the last but certainly the hardest.

♋

The seventh loss ended the cycle and gave way for me to have the children I desired. I carried my second child to the end of my 34th week and then I was so sick in my body that they had to induce labor and everyone thought the worst. To everyone's surprise, Camden came out fighting and screaming at 5 pounds. My family rejoiced in the fact that I had enough faith in God to endure the pain and trust that God would grant the desires of my heart. This was a testimony in itself.

I may not have believed for a while, but God brought me back from that place and reminded me of my foundation. Four months after delivering Camden, my husband and I found out we were pregnant again and I didn't have a shadow of a doubt that our baby would not be born healthy.

Our son came on time at 37 weeks; he was just shy of 9 pounds, and the healthiest baby I could ever have seen. God gave us two beautiful daughters and a son to complete our family.

God broke me down so that I could be the salt of the earth and season others' lives. When I was in my darkest hour and questioning everything and rebuking God from my life, He did not give up on me, he had a mission for me and I had to be prepared. I take much joy in the fact that when it is time for me to go to Heaven, my seven children will be there waiting with open arms for mommy and I will embrace them all because they are loved.

In my heart, I have three children on this earth, but I do have a total of 10 children and know I am so blessed to have them. I was only able to get through this trial because of my faith and relationship with God. Although it is the most difficult thing to face and go through, you must keep going. There is a light at the end of the tunnel. God has a plan designed specifically for each of us; it is up to us to allow God to tell us His plan.

I know it is hard now, but time and communication with God is the only way. No man can take you to the place you need to go, just The Man Upstairs.

Christine Alexander, woman of God. Married for 10 years, she's a full-time college student, full-time mom, and full-time wife. She's from a military family and married to a service member in the Navy. She loves God and loves her family.

1 Matthew 5:13

Part Two

HOPE

When Joy Replaces Sorrow

By Robert E. Stephenson

Lord let me find within
Sunshine for my soul
Peace to let me live again
With reasonable control.

Let me rise anew each day
With courage and to spare
Lend a hand to thwart decay
Help others in despair!

Let the smile seen on my face
No longer mask my gloom
Chase away the slightest trace
Seeking to consume!

Let the words you give to me
Encourage others too
Setting ransomed spirits free
As you know I should do.

Let those of us who've borne this cross
Know that on yon morrow
There is gain in our loss
When joy replaces sorrow!

No More Tears

By Cindy Cross Brookshire

"I sought the Lord, and he answered me, and delivered
me from all my fears."[1]

I can look back and not cry.

I'm 52, and haven't seen a period for more than a year. I've weathered hot flashes, stray hairs and that over-the-top snippiness you get when someone leaves a cart blocking the last parking space on a rainy day. My body is telling me child bearing has ended, more than a decade after the miscarriages and live births that peopled a maternal journey of enormous highs and devastating lows.

☙

"Are you sure?" I asked the doctor at the clinic that first time. I explained that my husband was a cancer survivor and after four years of trying, we thought it wasn't possible.

"Positive," she confirmed.

I let it sink in. The nausea, the bloating, the headaches. I was going to have a baby.

And I did. Virginia Caroline came that hot summer, after ten frightening hours of labor that ended with a forceps delivery.

We were so happy! I quit my job, set up a freelance business and immersed myself in an ocean of breastfeeding and washing cloth diapers. I would be the perfect stay-at-home mom.

Then, in February 1987, when Carrie was nine-months-old, the nausea returned.

"The diaphragm works, but you have to take it out of the drawer," joked Dr. Bentrum. I made a note to ask for the one female doctor in the practice next time.

A second child!

This time I was going to do natural childbirth. No epidural, no forceps. I'd breastfeed both children, in tandem! I scoured back issues of *Mothering* magazine and contacted LaLeche League.

☙

Then one morning, it happened. There was bright red blood in my panties. Despite each blot of toilet paper, I was still spotting. I counted the fingers of both hands. I was only ten weeks – less than three months along. This can't be happening!

I tried to deny it, tried to relax and pray myself okay. But in a few hours I was doubled with intense cramps and bled so much, Martin couldn't mop up the bathroom before I was back again.

He took me to the emergency room with 11-month-old Carrie and all her baby paraphernalia in tow. I sat on a plastic chair in the waiting room, a thick towel folded inside my jeans. In time, a doctor examined me and told us it was normal for a miscarriage. Normal? I was scared out of my wits! I hadn't just lost a baby tooth or grown breasts. Those are normal passages of life. I was losing my *baby*! Couldn't he give me medicine to stop the contractions and somehow block the flow of blood? But he moved on to other patients, leaving us with a nurse who explained that I should see my doctor in the morning to schedule a D&C.

"What's that?" I asked.

She explained, "It's dilatation and curettage, a dilation of the opening of the cervix under anesthesia. The doctor would use a loop-shaped knife to scrape ...."

I shivered with one of those all over shakes that chatters your teeth.

"What are you shaking for? Are you cold?" she innocently asked.

"No," I said, unable to control the shakes. "I don't know, it's just happening."

She talked more words, but I couldn't hear them. I was watching Martin in the doorway. After a long time, he'd finally gotten Carrie settled to sleep in the stroller. His body was in the room with me, but his arm rocked the stroller in the hallway outside, where it was quieter.

He would look from her to me, then back again.

The nurse gave me a large pad to take the place of the blood-soaked towel, which she rinsed and then put in a plastic bag. And then we went home.

Throughout the night, I could feel what had sustained my baby's life bleeding out.

The next day the doctor did a sonogram and checked for a heartbeat, confirming that our baby was dead. Martin rarely cried, but he did then, and when he called our parents later, he told them "Cindy and I have suffered a miscarriage."

But I was the one who shuffled slowly into the hospital that afternoon, and up to radiology, where I changed into a cloth gown that opened at the back.

The young man who was to take an x-ray of my chest asked one last question while he made the final adjustments and went behind the lead divider.

"Is there any chance that you're pregnant?"

The words stabbed, cold as the metal plate I was pushed up against.

"No," I said.

He doesn't know, I convinced myself. They have to ask questions like this.

In the operating room the anesthesia made my mouth taste like a metal car bumper, and then, just as quickly, I was in the recovery room. While I lay in a fog of drugs and despair, I listened to two orderlies discussing the best place to buy a VCR.

I wanted to jump up and smash their monitoring machines against the wall and yank down their clean white curtains and scream until the breath left my body:

"My baby is dead!"

But instead, I lay trapped in the body that had betrayed me. When I went back to the doctor for a follow-up visit, he rattled off statistics and percentages. The words clattered about his office like broken ivory keys on an old piano at a mountain lodge, tinny, muffled, harpy and wheezy.

My ears rang.

◌

Martin buried himself in his work. We suffered alone, not together. My parents came all the way from Nebraska to visit for 10 days. It was early spring, but they burst in with all the excitement of a regular summer visit. They laughed and played and hugged Carrie and showered her with attention. They took lots of pictures of her clapping and kissing cheeks.

I wanted to talk to my mom, really talk to her. But she'd never lost a child and her face turned red if you tried to talk about personal things. She felt more comfortable cooking and cleaning and fussing about. When they left, I felt even more alone.

I cried and stopped breastfeeding.

I'm ashamed now, when I look back on it. I know it was wrong to push my own child away, but I just couldn't take the intimacy of being that close to Carrie. It didn't take long for my milk to dry up. Carrie didn't even fuss. She loved drinking from her new yellow TommeeTippee cup.

Things went downhill. I missed writing deadlines. The house was dirty and unkempt. Martin and I argued. I didn't want to make love. I had a hard time eating or sleeping. Then, one morning at breakfast, we were fighting and I threw the TommeeTippee cup at Martin – right in front of Carrie.

That's when I sought help. Our Episcopal church rector told me about Gayle and her husband, who lost a child to stillbirth years before, and now ran a perinatal loss support group that met once a month at the church. On the appointed night, I went, and sat in a circle of metal chairs in the parish hall with other women or couples who had gone through miscarriages, stillbirth or infant loss.

Gayle facilitated the group, which meant she listened and passed the tissue box around when someone started crying. Lots of us started crying. Any person, who wanted to, could tell their story. I went home that night with many stories in my head, and each meeting added more. But I didn't want to say my private pain out loud, and have it become someone else's story, to be collected and carried away.

As I became more comfortable, I started to talk, and with talk, I started to cry. I told them about the time, a few days before the miscarriage, when I was rushing up the stairs from the laundry room with a diaper pail. I stepped over the child safety gate but the front of my shoe caught on it, and down I went, diaper pail and all. I lay there, feeling stupid, and then moved slowly to make sure I didn't break anything.

I asked the group, "Did the fall kill my baby?"

No one had the answer, but it was such a relief, to say my fear aloud. I felt lighter when I left that meeting, and went back many times.

"What is it you wanted to tell your mother?" Gayle prompted at one meeting.

"I needed to tell her how I felt," I said. "I wanted her to know my pain, without trying to fix it."

"How is your relationship with your husband?" she asked another time.

"Much better," I replied. "He's told me how it was for him, feeling so helpless. And I understand now he grieves in a different way."

The group was my safe place to let out my feelings, from anger and regret, to tears. Sometimes I started crying even before Gayle's husband had brought in the worn box full of loaner books, or pulled the chairs in a circle. After a year of going to the group, I felt better, like I didn't need to tell my story anymore. It was hard to witness the fresh tears of the newer people and bear their sadness. I don't know how Gayle could do it. I needed to stop going.

Then, two years after the miscarriage, when I was 34, my body switched over to babymaking again. We were overjoyed, even if the morning sickness came at a bad time: we were about to take a trip to London.

In my sixth week of pregnancy, we flew over the bottomless ocean, landed at Heathrow and plunged into the Underground. Once again, we were a happy little family on the move. On the last day, we took a train all the way to Windsor and toured the castle.

Inside, we came upon the tomb of a teenage princess – Charlotte

— who had died in childbirth. A stone angel carried her stillborn child heavenward. That's when I let the truth sink in. It was happening again. I'd been spotting for days, and my second miscarriage was on its way. Martin knew. Earlier, he'd asked if we should cut the trip short and go home.

"Why?" I asked. The blood didn't scare me this time. We were no longer strangers to loss.

Six days after we returned home, the cramps started and I miscarried. I even considered just having our baby at home the natural way. But the doctor said a D&C was better, so nothing is left behind that might cause infection or other problems. But I bled so much wasn't most of the baby already gone? No, he said. After the D&C, he confirmed at least 90 percent of the placenta and baby was still in my womb.

I went back to Gayle's perinatal loss support group. I knew I had to get my feelings out, not let them fester. I recognize depression now, as that feeling of being weighted down and dark, even on the sunniest of days. I knew that living in depression impacted not just me, but my husband and my daughter. I needed help and I got it. There was Gayle and her husband, and the tattered box of books, and the tissues, making their way around the circle. Only the faces were different. It took another year of support before I felt ready to face life on my own again.

Then in 1990, when I was 36, and Carrie was 4, I became pregnant again.

I was seized with irrational fears. When was it going to happen this time? How could I keep my body from failing again? I fantasized running away to have our baby, safely dodging the grim reaper who had chosen our door twice before.

But instead, I went to a Bible study at our church on Tuesday mornings and prayed that I was going to carry this baby to term. I started walking around the neighborhood for one mile, then longer. I volunteered at my daughter's preschool and did anything to stay active and not dwell on my fears. I wanted to believe, and left that desire in the arms of God, knowing that He understood why my faith was so weak, and that He loved me anyway.

꘎

Then it happened. Suddenly we were in the new birthing center and my contractions were coming so close together I couldn't get enough oxygen. My legs were splayed up in the air and the nurse was barking at me NOT to push yet, when every cell of my body wanted to push HARD. Martin leaned too close to me and I pulled his shirt in a knot and screamed, "Get your f---ing peanut butter breath out of my face!"

I thought I was dying. Here my baby was finally going to come into this world, and I would go right out of it.

But I survived and quickly, with a few pushes, James Willis was born. He was a healthy boy with a loud voice and after him, the doctor swore, the largest placenta he'd ever seen. I was so alive! I was holding my baby and it was bright sunlight and he was alive, with 10 pink fingers and 10 pink toes!

It's been more than 15 years since that day.

꘎

I wrote about my experiences for several reasons: To give you hope. To let you know that what you feel is familiar to others who have lost a child. To encourage you to seek at least one person you can talk to so you don't go through this alone.

I can't fix what happened to you. I can't make it better. But in the company of others, I know your pain, I acknowledge it, and I invite you to speak it out loud and take the first step on a journey of healing.

I've suffered more losses since then – the deaths of both my parents and, too early, Martin, at age 44. I like to think that he is with our two children in Heaven while I have been busy here, raising Carrie and Jamie. I'm now joined in that commitment by Curtis, who had given up on ever finding a wife or having children – until he met us.

Some people think miscarriages are not the same as losing a baby at full term or after birth. To me, the loss is just as deep. I think we are all part of God's creation, no matter how long we live – 10 weeks, 52 years, or longer.

And oh, how I thank God for the blessings of this life!

Cindy Cross Brookshire is a writer, a widow who remarried, and "home base" for two teenagers in Manassas, Virginia. She works with youth at Trinity Episcopal Church.

1 Psalm 34:4 (NASB)

LEARNING TO LIVE
AFTER LOSING AN ANGEL

By Suzan Wells

"He heals the brokenhearted and binds up their wounds."[1]

It *seemed* like a normal morning. I gave my 15-month-old daughter a kiss, said "I love you" then walked out the door. That was the last time I saw Cierra alive.

I stayed at the babysitter's that night because I had to be at work early the next morning. While I did my hair, I prepared a cup of Cheerios to keep Cierra busy. I rushed out the door to work and my heart crumbles when I think of what happened next.

It was February 26, 2002 and in the middle of a delivery at work, I received a call from a co-worker telling me to get back to the store. When I arrived, I was told I needed to contact Cierra's babysitter. The sitter said Cierra had choked on Cheerios and stopped breathing. I dropped everything and raced to the emergency room at UC Davis Medical Center.

"My daughter, Cierra, was brought here. Where is she?" I demanded. It seemed like forever, but only a few minutes passed when the nurse came back with another person. I did not know who or what the person was, but I continued to ask about Cierra. They both led me to a little room.

A few minutes later, a doctor came in and began speaking in a low, calm voice. He mentioned "sudden death." As soon as I heard the word *death*, I lost it. Not my Cierra with her big brown eyes and angel curls. I thought of her twirling to her favorite movie, *Shrek*. I could hear her baby voice trying to form words and how I couldn't help but smile when

I saw her. She was so full of personality, so full of life. I could still see Cierra holding her bottle with her feet, like a cute little chimp would! I had just seen her this morning. I could not believe *my* angel was dead. I felt like someone took a sledge hammer to my heart and smashed it. I couldn't hear anything the doctor said after that report.

"I want to see my daughter," I cried. He agreed and led me to her. She was lying in the emergency room on a gurney, not moving. All I could do was hold her and cry. Seeing her lifeless body was the hardest thing in the world, but now I had to do the second hardest thing. I called my dad and stepmother, who I had lived with for the first nine months of Cierra's short life. I had to tell them she was gone. I didn't know what to say so I cried and mumbled, "She's gone."

The hospital allowed me to take Cierra to another room. When my dad and stepmother arrived, I was sitting in disbelief. I held Cierra in my arms and thought, h*ow could this happen to such an innocent little girl?* My dad scooped up Cierra then laid her on the bed and talked prayed quietly over her. He was in shock and to this day still hasn't dealt with her loss.

The hospital chaplain came in to talk with us. He was sorry for the loss of my daughter and he gave us names of groups that could help us get through this tragedy. At the time, I felt like no one could possibly know what I was going through or even understand.

I struggled with feelings of confusion, frustration, and loneliness. Although overwhelmed with despair, I still had to call Cierra's dad, Ronnie. When we spoke, I could not say the word "dead" because it hurt too much.

෨

The next day, I was at the babysitter's house when a couple of detectives asked me to go to the police station and give a statement about the morning Cierra died. I went with them and told them what I did that day. They asked me what I knew about my babysitter's son, Maurice. I knew he had just been released from jail a few months ago. Maurice said he was in jail for burglary and now had a job at a hotel. The police said Maurice was actually in prison for armed robbery and child abuse. The next thing I knew, the police had gone to pick Maurice up from the hotel and I was left dumbfounded.

Had I known he was convicted of such crimes, I would never have left my daughter there, but it was too late. I felt so guilty because I did not make sure he was telling me the truth. I agonized over all the "what if" scenarios.

If only I did a little research, Cierra would still be here. If only I would have called in sick that morning. If only, if only, if only! I was so upset, I could barely speak. Once I calmed down, the police gave me a ride back to the babysitter's house. Ronnie was there waiting. We had taken a walk to talk about what happened. We hadn't seen each other in a while and he had only seen Cierra four times the entire time she was alive, but had the nerve to threaten me.

"You better not have had anything to do with Cierra being killed," he accused. I was devastated. I screamed back at him, "You have no right to say anything to me; you were not there for her!"

I was doing everything on my own. I did the best I could and he dared to criticize – to accuse me! He apologized and tried to calm me down. When I felt composed, I told him what the detectives said about Maurice. Ronnie had a few days before he had to go back to work and there was still so much to do.

I was still in shock. I had to call around to price a funeral for my angel. It was so hard. Cierra should be doing this for me, not the other way around! We decided to have Cierra cremated, that way I could always keep an eye on her. No one would ever harm her again. At the funeral home we signed papers to have Cierra's body released from the hospital. A tear ripped through my heart with every stroke of the pen. I felt like crawling in a hole and never coming out.

From there we went to the coroner's office to pick up the blue topaz stud earrings Cierra wore the day she died. When I saw the earrings, I felt like I was repeating history back in the hospital room. I just wanted to die, too.

Ronnie and I went back to the hotel room so I could rest. I felt so tired and worn out. I didn't want to do anything. I didn't want to talk to anyone. I only wanted to die. I slithered into the bed and cried myself to sleep. The next day, I awakened and thought all of this was a nightmare, but it wasn't. I saw Ronnie and started to cry again.

၅

That day we had to talk to the district attorney about what was going to happen from here. The DA said the coroner found bruising around Cierra's mouth which meant this was no choking accident, but she had been smothered. The police arrested Maurice for Cierra's murder and a hearing for the trial date would be scheduled the following week. The DA also gave me the number to Victims of Violent Crimes to help me pay Cierra's bills and to get counseling.

The next day Ronnie had to leave. When he left, I felt even more alone. I didn't know how to talk to my dad about how I was feeling. My dad is a retired soldier from the old Army. He taught me to deal with my feelings and move on so I never learned how to express my emotions, but I did know how to put up a façade.

So, instead of talking about my anguish, I decided to go back to work. I worked as much as I could because work became my way of escape. After work, I couldn't eat or sleep and when I finally did get to sleep, I didn't want to wake up. On my next day off from work, I decided to call The Victims of Violent Crimes to see what they could do to help. They assigned a counselor who they thought could help through my grief. I went and saw her once a week for a month. While seeing the counselor, I learned that Maurice's trial would be set for July. I thought the counseling was effective, so believed I would be able to handle attending the trial on my own.

The trial was a week away when the DA called to say the trial would be postponed until September. I was heartbroken. I was having a hard enough time keeping myself together and I was getting close to losing it.

About a month later, I was at work and overheard a conversation between two co-workers. They were talking about not being able to see their kids even though they paid child support. That comment bothered me so much I could not keep my mouth shut.

I blurted, "At least you have a choice about whether to see your kids. I will never see my daughter again!"

I realized that was the first time I admitted aloud that Cierra was dead. Nick, the guy who I interrupted, came up to me a few days later and asked if there was anything he could do and if I ever needed to talk he would listen. One night we went out for coffee and I told him what I was going through. From there we hit it off. Finally, there was someone interested in how I felt. It felt so good! Nick introduced me to his family who invited me to church. Through Nick and his family, I learned that it is okay to talk about how you feel and express your innermost feelings.

During this time, I also realized that God did not do this to Cierra and that she is with God who is watching over me. She really is okay.

☽

The trial was a few days away when the DA called.

"The case has been transferred to a new DA and the trial will be pushed back to January," he said. It seemed like Cierra was never going to get her justice! Cierra's birthday was coming up December 3 and I was feeling more and more in the dumps. I missed her so much. She would have been two years old. A strong feeling of depression began to take over, but Nick helped me get through by letting me cry on his shoulder and he held me whenever I needed it. On Cierra's birthday and again at the one year anniversary of her death, Nick took me to the park to release balloons. I needed her to know that she is in our hearts, we'll always be thinking about her, and we're still seeking justice.

January 2003 passed, then March, then October. Still no trial. Again, I thank God for Nick and his family for they helped me get through postponement after postponement after postponement. I became pregnant again and five months later, Nick and I were married. I was so happy. I had not felt like this since my daughter was alive. When I learned I was pregnant, it forced me to start taking care of myself again. I knew this was a new opportunity for me to begin to heal. I was wrong.

I was still feeling stressed, wondering if December would be the final date or if the trial would be postponed again. I wanted this monster to finally pay for what he had done to my angel, Cierra!

◌

On October 7, I had my son a month early. When I saw him, I didn't want to let him out of my sight. I was determined not to allow anyone to hurt him the way his sister was hurt. I know I was overprotective, but I was not going to lose another child. I couldn't trust anyone with my son. Almost three years later, I still can't let him out of my sight when other people are around.

When I had to go back to work it was extremely painful. My mother-in-law babysat for me, but I would call to see how my son was doing every hour or two. Up until he became Cierra's age, I was very paranoid. I felt anxious when, as a baby, he slept with me and my husband. I would wake up every 30 to 45 minutes to check on him thinking he was getting squished by Nick although I slept between them.

In my eyes I'm as normal as I can be after what I've gone through. I don't think I'll ever fully trust someone watching my son, but I'll have to let that go so he can grow up and be a healthy kid. I understand that is still an area of weakness for me. I don't want to trap him in a bubble because I'm afraid something might happen to him.

December finally arrived, and the trial was about to begin. I was nervous. I had to relive that dreaded day all over again. The memories were so painful. I started crying and when it was my turn to speak, it was hard to deliver the story. I had a hard time reading what I wrote to him. My leg was shaking like you wouldn't believe, I had tears rolling down my face and the first lines didn't come out clear. I was so nervous and anxious to tell Maurice what I wanted to tell him. No matter how much hate I felt at the beginning, it was pointless now. There was nothing that would bring Cierra back. I just missed her and wanted her back. I couldn't believe what he had done to her.

The trial lasted a week and the jury was out for a day and a half. The courts found Maurice guilty on two counts of murder. I was so happy that Maurice would pay for what he did to my daughter. The courts then set a date for a sentencing trial. On that day, the courts allowed me to address my angel's murderer.

"I do not understand how you could do this to Cierra. She was a very beautiful and loving girl. Her big brown eyes and curly hair brought a smile to everyone she met. Now she cannot bring that joy to anyone, anymore. Even though I will never hear her call me "mommy," and she will never get to know her brother or the rest of the family, it is okay because I know she is in a better place. Cierra is in a place where no one like you can hurt her anymore. She smiles down on us with love and happiness. Knowing that, and needing to be strong for my son and Cierra, I can say this with a lifted heart; justice has prevailed and I forgive you. God will judge you and I will never forget."

After I had my say, the judge gave Maurice his sentence. He received 50 years to life in prison. When I heard that sentence come out of the judge's mouth, I whispered a little message to Cierra saying, "We did it baby, the monster is paying for what he did to you. You can be at peace now."

When the second anniversary of Cierra's death came around, I decided to celebrate it as a rebirth into God's kingdom, instead of making that day a mark of her death. She is in a better place looking down at us, with God. I also knew I would be with her when the time was right. I wanted to remember how loving and beautiful she was and how she loved to laugh and dance around the room. For the next year, I focused on the happy memories instead of everything I'll miss about being her mom. It took me a long time to get rid of those what if questions, but it was going to drown me if I kept going like that. I still have bad days, especially when my son makes the same expression Cierra used to make when she wanted something. My mother-in-law talked me into going to see another counselor because I still carried severe grief.

I left my emotional wall at the door and started talking about how I truly felt. I started from the beginning and tried to explain how I felt when everything happened. I had been carrying this burden and holding everything in for so long. I was relieved to finally let it all out. There is no real way to grieve, but until I was ready and willing to open up and allow someone to help me, true healing couldn't begin.

In April of 2005, after three months of counseling, I finally felt like

I was no longer the victim and it was not my fault Cierra died. God has a plan for me to share what I overcame with other families. I'm finally ready to let the healing begin.

Suzan Wells is a stay-at-home mom of a two-year-old son and the wife of an Army soldier. She has an A. A. S. in drafting and is a designer of unique, handmade soaps and gift baskets for any occasion.

HOPING FOR A BRIGHTER DAY

By Jacqueline A. Toon

"I will never leave you or forsake you."[1]

As a soldier, people think I'm supposed to be tough but I hurt, too. I hope and pray and yearn for things lost. I hope my story will touch someone and give hope and understanding.

When my water broke November 30, I was 26 weeks pregnant and asked myself why this happened. And why did it happen to *me*? My husband rushed me to the hospital and I told myself *it's too soon* but also tried to reassure myself that everything would be fine. I was airlifted to Vanderbilt University Hospital, the best trauma hospital in Tennessee, so I knew they'd take good care of me.

I spent the next two weeks at Vanderbilt, but when I hit 28 weeks, the doctors noticed my baby, Mia, was starting to show signs of an infection. They put me on the monitor to track her heartbeat, but on December 12, 2005 they decided to deliver our baby. I had an emergency C-section under general anesthesia, so I never got to see my baby girl.

I woke up to a nurse telling me, "Your daughter isn't doing too well. We have to give her blood." This was only the first of many horrible announcements the staff would make that day.

The nurse came back a second time, a few hours later.

"Mrs. Toon, do you want to see your daughter? It looks like she's not going to make it." I couldn't believe what she was saying to me. I had faith that God would make everything alright. I went to see my little Mia in the neonatal intensive care unit.

"Mrs. Toon your baby's heart rate never got above 120 and we are helping her to breathe," the doctor said.

"You have to make the decision to take her off the breathing machine," he added. Those words hung in the air; their heaviness weighed me down. This was the hardest thing I had to do. This wasn't happening; I was in somebody else's bad dream. This is not my reality.

I held my child in my arms while she passed away.

&

I couldn't take this anymore. I went back to my room, my heart breaking in a thousand pieces wondering what I did wrong, why my child? I would have been a great mother. I have all the love in the world to give my daughter.

The nurses asked if I wanted them to dress Mia and bring her to me. I said yes because that was going to be the only time I'd have to spend with my daughter.

I held her in my arms and checked her toes and fingers. I stared in amazement at her perfect nose and how smooth her black hair felt. I held Mia to my chest for hours. I don't know how long, but time didn't register. I was with my daughter and that's all that mattered at that moment.

My husband was going through his own private hell. He wanted his little girl more than anything in the world. He would tell me, "I can't wait for her to get here; she's going to be my baby, you'll see." He felt like his dream was snatched from him. I had never seen my husband cry like this, and know this was his greatest loss.

While we were holding our baby, he just repeated over and over; "Why did this have to happen to us? Just a few hours ago, I was looking in her eyes and she was looking in my eyes. What did I do to deserve this?" The crying went on for hours before we decided to let them take our baby back. It felt like we were living a dream. A dream we never thought could happen to us.

The second day for me was the hardest because all I wanted was to take my baby home and bury her. The staff asked if we wanted her cremated. To me that wasn't an option. I couldn't stand the thought of Mia being burned, it just felt like she was in pain and it hurt my heart just to think of her body going through the fire.

I had to spend several days in the hospital before I could go home. This was torture for me. All I could do was lie there and look at the nurses' faces. Their expressions said they wanted to say something, but didn't want to upset me.

◌

The funeral was very tough but I had my close friends and family there. They pulled me through the day because I was a mess. I hardly remember anything. I can remember them putting my baby's little white casket in the ground and I thought, *she should be in my belly right now.*

How can life be so cruel? Why me? What did I do wrong? The truth is, I didn't do anything wrong and yet I couldn't help feeling like I was being punished.

I was surrounded by my family, but there were days when I just wanted them to go away and stop asking me if I was doing okay. My mother hovered around me, but that's what mothers do when their children are in pain.

I just wanted to yell at her and force her to tell me what to do and how to feel. I asked how I could deal with something like this. She said, "Only God can help, have faith and keep praying." I don't want to have faith right now! Instead I want to lay down in self pity.

Many times, I counted the passing days and weeks and said to myself, *today she would be a week old and she should be lying on my stomach and crying.* I would yearn to hear her cry and all I could think was, *I didn't get to see her full of life and looking around.*

Some days I still find myself weeping aloud. I cry for my child when no one is around because it is easier when I can be myself and scream and ask God, *why me?* The truth is, I don't know why this happened to me and sometimes wonder if this is some kind of test or cruel joke. When is this nightmare going to be over?

If this is a test of my faith, I wonder how I am going to overcome. I look at this grieving process as a day-by-day survival, you either sink or swim. When you think your grief will overpower you, have faith and understand it won't always be like this. I often bounce back and forth between having faith and losing it. I always get it back though.

◦

I think I was little resentful towards God because I would look around and see all the pregnant women. I would say to myself, *I should be pregnant right now.* Sometimes it felt like I was drowning in a river and I couldn't come up for air because everywhere I looked babies surrounded me.

I would watch television and all commercials were about pregnant women or about babies. This was too much to bear. I just wanted to crawl in a ball and never get out of bed. I had to press on because if I gave in one day then it would be another day and before I knew it weeks would have passed. I still blame myself a little bit and don't know if I will ever stop, but I'm working on it one day at a time.

The hardest part was going back to work and facing all those people who had this look of pity on their faces. I knew they wanted to say something but didn't know what to say. I just wanted to scream and say, "I just lost my child, you idiots! Just say I'm sorry about the loss of your child even if you don't mean it."

This is where the pretending starts. Even now, I try to put on a brave face and pretend I am fine; all the while my heart is breaking into little pieces. Everybody expects me to be the same person who left a couple of months ago. The truth is I will never be that same person.

This is my hardest journey and sometime I feel like I'm going to have a nervous breakdown. I have to muddle my way to the surface of my despair and tell myself, *hold on Jackie you can make it another day.*

◦

I never knew how much my child would touch my life even though she's been in my stomach and I never saw her before her birth. The bond is so great. I miss her so much. I will share some of the feelings you might experience if you have just lost a baby.

The first couple hours is going to be a blur if you are going through a similar situation. Just hold on to your faith and pray and look at the good things in your life. I know it's going to be hard because all you want to do is lay in that bed and anguish over all the bad things and ask

God, *why me?*

You can ask why but don't let the hurt and pain eat you alive. Call a friend or a family member to be with you. Try not to be alone. Surround yourself with positive people and don't allow yourself to fall into despair.

I know you're going to want to lie down and not get up, but you have to. If you have other children, focus on them. Make sure you get pictures of your baby so you can remember what he or she looks like.

Talk about your child because your baby is a real person and don't pretend they never existed. That will hurt more than anything. Force the people around you to talk about your child, too. Some people will avoid talking about your baby because they are afraid of hurting you. Tell them, it does hurt, but avoiding the subject only hurts more.

There were even times when I felt like leaving my marriage. Just walking away and never looking back. I thought I would be better off by myself. Not everybody will feel that way, but I did. If you're feeling this way, and your marriage is worth fighting for, stand and fight. Please don't give up on it.

Try not to get obsessed with having another baby. This is how desperate I've become. I told my husband I would not make love to him if he wouldn't consider having another child. If that's not a sign of a person losing her mind, I don't what it is!

Remember that communication is the key. Don't get all wrapped up in thoughts of your child and think you are the only one who's hurting. Not so. Friends, family members and your significant other are hurting, too. My friend and I were pregnant at the same time and our due dates were only a couple of days apart. She just had her baby three months ago. Our friendship started to feel weird after my loss.

We would always call each other at least three or four times a week, but after she had the baby, we hardly ever talked. It felt like she was shutting me out and this made me feel worse than ever. I couldn't take any more; it was tearing me up inside because we always had been close. I called her recently and we had a long talk. I explained that she doesn't have to feel bad around me because I lost my baby and she didn't. I want to hear about her baby and her life. This talk made both of us feel better and I'm happy that I made that phone call. Communication really is so important!

I've gone to a counselor and she thinks I should move on. I don't think she knows how hard it is, so I just quit going. People think just because I'm a soldier I should get over my loss and move on. What they don't understand is that I'm human first and I have weaknesses and shortcomings.

It's only been five months since I lost my child, so you can see this is very raw for me and I'm still going through the healing process. I suffer from nightmares and dreams of holding my child only to wake and she's not here with me. I can't even bring myself to get rid of her things, because, in my mind, getting rid of her stuff is like saying I don't want to acknowledge that she ever existed.

It's a daily struggle for me and my husband, but we're taking one baby step at a time. My mother always says it's not going to rain forever, the sun is going to shine again. Together, we'll see that a brighter day is coming and we'll soon smell the flowers again.

Jacqueline Toon is a soldier stationed at Fort Campbell, Kentucky. She's been in the Army for 19 years and will retire next year. Her military career has taken her to Panama, Georgia, Korea and Germany. She is married to a retired soldier and is the mother of a 14-year-old son.

Hebrews 13:5

Destination Heaven

By Amber Beardsley

*"It's better to have loved and lost than never to have
loved at all."*[1]

It had been a very long and stressful month for my husband and me. We literally made love one time the entire month. It just happened to be the right time to get pregnant.

Since it had been more than a year of trying and fertility testing showed my husband had a very low sperm count, we just assumed it couldn't happen "by accident." Maybe we were naïve, but that is what we really thought.

It was Tuesday, February 28, 2006 and I had been feeling sick. I figured I would get a pregnancy test just to put my mind at ease. Because I was so sure it would come back negative and I would start my period at any time, I almost didn't buy it. I thought it would be a waste of money; something that is definitely a rarity when a family of five lives on one low salary.

I took the test as soon as I got home. I stood there in shock as the dark plus sign quickly appeared. My shaky palms felt sweaty. I thought to myself, this can't be happening. What are we going to do? Our youngest son wasn't five-months-old yet!

I must have stood in the bathroom for a good five or 10 minutes staring at the little plus sign, hoping it would disappear any second. I finally realized this was happening. I was really pregnant, again.

How would I tell my husband?

❧

"Well I don't have the flu," I told my husband, Rob.

"Oh really, how do you know?" He innocently asked. I dropped the bomb.

"Because I'm pregnant."

I will never forget the look on his face as he said, "You're what? How did that happen? Are you sure?" If I wasn't still shocked, I probably would have laughed until I cried.

I constantly wondered what we would do. How were we going to afford another baby? Rob planned to get out of the Army and go to school in January of 2007. We had planned that I was going to get a job and support the family until he got his schooling out of the way but how was I going to do that now? I was due in early November.

We told both our parents the next day. His dad was excited about having another grandbaby but worried about my health. I had hemorrhaged a lot after giving birth to Caleb. As a family, we came up with a financial plan. It wasn't going to be easy, but it was doable. I felt a little bit better after that.

As the days passed I started to feel excited. I was beginning to look forward to having another baby. Rob and I had started talking about names and about whether we wanted another boy or a girl. We both really wanted to have a daughter since we already had three sons. I dreamed of frilly dresses and the long mother and daughter talks we would have when she grew older. Maybe we'd even have a close relationship like what my mom and I share.

The best part was going to be that my husband would be there. He missed Caleb's birth because he was deployed and couldn't hold him until he was 6-weeks-old. I never in a million years thought there was the slightest possibility I would lose my baby. I never had issues with past pregnancies, why would this be any different?

Fast forward to Saturday, March 11. We had just finished dinner at my in-laws house when I noticed something was wrong. I went to the bathroom and there was just the tiniest amount of blood on the toilet paper. It wasn't enough to get on my underwear, but it was still there.

I felt a little shaken but I didn't get super freaked out because Rob and I had made love the night before. I heard it wasn't unusual to spot afterwards. It wasn't as if I experienced cramping or anything. This never happened to me before, but there is a first time for everything and every pregnancy is different, so they say. I decided to keep an eye on the spotting and if it grew worse or lasted too long, I would get checked out. I told Rob about the spotting, but told him not to worry – yet. That evening, I must have gone to the bathroom like 20 times just to check. It didn't get any worse but it was definitely still there. I still didn't have cramping, but was starting to feel more worried.

○

Sunday I spent most of the day in bed. The bleeding grew a little worse, but my mom said I should just rest and see my doctor the next day especially since there was no cramping. I tried to sleep but cried instead. Why was this happening to me? What did I do wrong?

That evening after dinner I couldn't take it any more. I had to know what was going on inside my body, so I went to the emergency room. The wait seemed to take forever, but finally it was my turn. The doctor ordered a blood test to check my hormone levels. I was almost six weeks pregnant and the level was at the low end of the normal range at 1,300. He did a pelvic exam and said that my cervix was still closed and thought the bleeding came from cervical trauma after having sex during the past 72 hours.

Later, Rob and I went for an ultrasound. The technician was nice; she pointed to what were the beginnings of fetal parts. Seeing the baby started to put my mind at ease.

Forty-eight hours later, I had more blood drawn to determine my hormone levels. The first blood test came back at 1,444. The number had increased, but not anywhere near doubling like they told me it should. At that point I was pretty sure that I had lost the baby. I was near hysteria. I wanted to get it over with. Everyone told me that it was going to be okay, the number had still increased; I should wait and see the results of the next blood test.

Wednesday I was actually starting to feel better. The bleeding wasn't as bad and I still never had cramping so I figured that everything would be okay.

Thursday, March 16 I had the next blood test. My hormone levels had not doubled; instead they plummeted to 274! There was no way to avoid admitting the inevitable at that point. I went outside and thought this had to be wrong. It was so unfair! I didn't think I had any tears left in me. I was angry.

It was such a beautiful day, the sun was shining and the sky was blue without a cloud in sight. I heard the birds chirping and wondered how it could be so beautiful when I had just heard the worst thing that a woman can hear? It felt like God was mocking me.

The next day, Rob cringed as the doctor put the referral into the computer. Spontaneous abortion. It seems like such a cold term. Like I had just up and decided I didn't want my baby when in reality like a train wreck, my world had just crashed. I had spent many hours praying that everything would be okay. I even prayed for God to let me live just long enough to give birth and then take me instead of our baby.

The doctor interrupted my thoughts to say he was sorry. He also instructed me to quit smoking, that maybe it was part of the reason I had lost my baby.

☙

The OB/GYN was one of the nicest people I have ever met. The first thing she said was it wasn't my fault our baby died and she hugged me. She told me it wasn't because I smoked, ate the wrong foods or because of sex or anything else. She said that the only way it could have possibly been my fault is if I had been doing cocaine, which of course I wasn't.

She said it was okay to grieve my loss, but I shouldn't feel guilty.

"It just wasn't meant to be," the OB/GYN doctor said.

It just wasn't meant to be? Those have to be the emptiest words I have ever heard in my entire life. I know that she meant to comfort me, but it wasn't any comfort at all. I wanted to know why. Why did I lose my baby, why did she have to die? Unfortunately, I will never have an answer to that question. The best answer I heard was that it could have been a chromosomal defect upon conception, but there was still no way to tell for sure.

The doctor was going to monitor my hormone levels until they dropped to "not pregnant" anymore. She explained that a level of five or less was basically as good as zero and meant that my body had metabolized the pregnancy hormone.

So basically, I wasn't pregnant any more, but my body didn't know yet. I had so many questions and so few answers. I felt empty and like I wasn't a woman anymore. How could I be a woman and not be able to carry a baby? I was a failure. Worse yet I had so many emotions floating around. I felt guilty. I thought this was my fault because when I first found out I was pregnant I wasn't happy. I didn't want to be pregnant at first, so God was teaching me a lesson. But most of all I was angry. How could God do this to me? He gave me something I didn't even know I wanted then took it back.

I was raised to believe that God never gives you more than you can handle, but how was I going to survive? I would never get to see my baby, never get to hold her or hear the first words or the first giggles and coos. I wanted to crawl into a corner and die. I didn't see how I would ever get over this. All I could see was the darkness, the tragedy. I didn't want to eat; all I wanted was to sleep and pretend that this wasn't happening to me. I was mad as hell and I didn't care who knew it.

Rob tried to tell me he understood how I felt and he was there for me if I wanted to talk. I didn't see how he could possibly understand; and further, how could he not be crying? Our baby died and nothing I did was good enough; I couldn't save her. I felt so helpless.

I was sick of hearing how sorry everyone was and how they understood what I was going through. They couldn't possibly understand. My mom finally made me snap out of it in a way. She told me I wasn't the only one going through this. She said I couldn't shut out my husband; and he lost a baby too. My husband *didn't* understand though. He told me I needed to cry. I couldn't get him to understand that I didn't have any tears left. All I felt was anger; I was mad at God.

The hardest part is not having a place to go to feel close to my child. There is no grave to visit and place flowers. It's as though she never existed. But I know she did; she is in my heart and always will be. I don't know if the pain will ever completely go away but it does lessen with each passing day. At times I feel guilty because I can go a few days without thinking about what happened. But, I have to be strong because I have three sons that need their mother.

I don't know if I will ever have another child, the doctors assure me that I can. My reason for not knowing if I will try again has nothing to do with fear. I am no longer afraid of losing another child; it is a question of what is right for my family. We had already decided before I got pregnant that we were done having children and my husband was going to have a vasectomy.

*

It took weeks for me to come around completely. I still don't understand why it had to happen and don't think I ever will, but I have the beginnings of peace in my heart. I am not a person that opens up easily to many people, but the best thing I did was to start talking to my husband.

It took awhile, but finally I completely broke down and sobbed while he held me. I didn't feel so alone after that. I just couldn't hold it all inside or I would lose my sanity. I'm not alone although many times it seemed that way. In many ways, my husband and I are much closer and our relationship is stronger for having gone through this together. Of course that will never make up for what we have lost but it is somewhat of a consolation.

I knew I couldn't cry forever or crawl into a corner and die, but it was okay for me to have those feelings. It was normal to be sad and angry all at the same time. Even though I lost my baby at six weeks, she was still real to me and I'm still entitled to grieve her passing. I still don't know how I will make it when her due date comes, but I learned that all you can do is live your life as it comes at you.

The best thing that I ever did, though, was talk about my experience. I opened up and shared my deepest darkest thoughts and feelings. Once they were out there, they didn't seem so big and bad.

I have been blessed many times over in my life. I choose to focus on those blessings. I am lucky to have my children and husband and each time I hug or kiss or just look at them, I'm reminded that life is precious.

The best advice I could give someone who has lost a child is to grieve but realize your life must go on. Know that no matter how bad it seems now, keep moving forward and you will survive. Never let anyone tell you what to feel because only you know what you need to heal.

It is okay to be angry and sad and everything in between. It is also okay to laugh and to smile. Don't feel guilty for those things. There is no set or right amount of time to grieve. It may take one person days, but the next person might need years. Neither is wrong. Just take it one day at a time.

Amber Beardsley is a stay-at-home mom originally from Cuyahoga Falls, Ohio. She moved to Clarksville, Tennessee after marrying her best friend of 10 years, a soldier, assigned to Fort Campbell, Kentucky. She is mother to three wonderful boys and an angel.

1 Lord Alfred Tennyson

HIS GRACE AND STRENGTH
SEE ME THROUGH

By Tedianne Toyllens

*"Therefore David said to his servants, 'Is the child
dead?' And they said, 'He is dead.' So David arose from
the ground, washed and anointed himself, and changed
his clothes; and he went into the house of the Lord and
worshiped."[1]*

People can't seem to understand why women can get so attached to a
little "thing" in just a few weeks time. The person who can't understand
this probably has not thought deeply about the awesome wonder of a
life growing inside of them. Some might feel compelled to shout the
news of their pregnancy from the mountain tops, but I kept this news
to myself.

We just had a tragic loss in our family so I felt sad saying goodbye to
this family member, but found a glimmer of comfort when I thought of
the circle of life. We'd be adding another one before the year ended.

The moment I found out I was pregnant, my outlook changed. My
plans for the future now included a new life for which I'd be responsible.
I couldn't help dreaming and wondering what joys and experiences this
new life would bring.

A few short months later, everything drastically changed again. After
a series of sonograms, the doctors determined my baby was unable to
grow because of a lack of fluid surrounding her. We felt traumatized and
discouraged, but my husband, Michael, and I determined to have faith
that things could change.

૭

Around the same time, a group of people at work began a new book study during our lunch break. They chose the book, "When God Doesn't Make Sense" by Dr. James Dobson. I have to admit, I decided to participate only out of curiosity.

I wondered how anyone could accuse God of not making sense! I couldn't join the group in person so decided to read on my own. WOW! Did I get the surprise of my life! Before reading this book, I always believed that if something bad happened it was probably because I had an area of sin that needed correction.

I used to think God was punishing me by complicating my pregnancy. This weight on my mind was slowly lifted as I delved deeper into the book. Each time I read a section from the book, it prepared me for the next gloomy prognosis from the doctor. Twice a month I saw a specialist and had a sonogram which updated us on the baby's status. During each visit, I received a blow to my soul when he said I probably wouldn't carry to full term. Continuing to hear this discouraging news four months straight really took its toll on me. I just couldn't understand why this was happening to me! Why would I not be given the opportunity to raise this child as part of our earthly family?

After an ultrasound at the end of July, the doctor said words we did not want to hear. He thought I would carry to full-term, but that my little girl would not have lungs. I was scheduled to attend a Woman of Faith convention that weekend and really didn't feel like being around a bunch of happy women when I was so sad inside. The anticipation of questions about the pregnancy and visions of women touching my belly made me want to scream! I knew with every question and every touch I would be reminded of the awful words the doctor spoke a few days before.

That night, as I lay in bed I shared my frustrations with Michael. He spoke kind words to encourage me. I believe the Holy Spirit gave me a revelation through my husband. He said, "Whether your baby lives or dies, My grace and strength will see you through." Those words were comforting to my soul, because the Lord was reminding me that although these circumstances were hard, God would see me through.

Just as I would trust the Lord for grace and strength to raise my little girl if she survived, I needed His grace and strength to see me through this ordeal. I decided I would attend the convention as planned. I'm sure glad I went. One of the speakers spoke about the faithfulness of the Lord. Her motto was, "Life is tough, but God is FAITHFUL!"

This gave me comfort beyond measure. I knew in my heart that the Lord did not want my baby to die. I knew beyond a shadow of doubt that the enemy comes to kill, steal, and destroy my faith, my baby and me, if he could! I also began to realize that as a Christian, I live in a world filled with evil. Just as the rain falls on the just and the unjust, evil will also touch Christians' lives from time to time. The difference between believers and non-believers is how we react to that evil, and I refused to give up on God.

Approximately two weeks after that convention I was on my way home from work and began to cry out to the Lord. I had a sonogram scheduled in two days, and to be honest, I felt weary of bad news. I told the Lord I knew He could heal my baby, but if that was not going to happen, I just didn't understand why I would have to go two more months under constant stress.

My Wednesday doctor's appointment arrived. After drinking all of the required water, I needed to use the restroom before the exam. Since I was alone, I began talking with the Lord.

"Lord, how should I react today when they tell me my baby has died?" I asked. At first I was mad at myself for thinking this, but peace came over me. There was no possible way I could have known our baby had died. Although I was 29 weeks along, Elizabeth was so very small and I could barely feel her movements.

During the sonogram the technician got a strange look on her face. She wouldn't say much except that she needed to get the doctor. As the doctor looked at the screen I could tell by the look on his face what he was about to say. Our baby girl was gone.

Michael and I began to weep. As long as she was still alive inside of me there was hope for a turnaround, but now all hope of survival was gone! We would not have the opportunity to hear our baby's cry, see her beautiful smile, or experience all the joy she would have brought to our family. They couldn't determine an exact date of death so they felt it was detrimental to my health to delay delivery. They scheduled the birth for the next day.

I went home after the ultrasound and still remember the rain that kept coming down. Although I listened to encouragement from our pastor and then a close friend; the sound of the rain comforted me most. To me, the Lord shed tears of sadness, because he knew how much his child was hurting. He wept with me.

We go through crazy emotions during times like these. I still remember hearing my husband on the phone with the youth pastor. Michael told him I "lost" the baby. I yelled from the other room, "I haven't lost the baby, I know where she is!"

And you know what? I do know where she is. She is in Heaven, she is perfect, and she is waiting to greet her daddy, her mother, and her big brother one day. In 2 Corinthians 1:3-4, the Bible says God will comfort us when we go through trials so we might be a comfort to others.

❧

I had a friend lose a baby almost a year before Elizabeth died. She came over and told me what to expect when they induced labor the next day. She shared pamphlets the hospital had given her and said she would have loved to have had the same information before her own delivery.

We are so used to seeing the beautiful bouncing babies after they are born. She wanted me to understand that my baby would not look that way because skin is one of the last things a baby develops.

I also learned that giving birth on the maternity floor where I could hear other babies crying would re-affirm my loss and help me through the "denial" stage of the grief process. Reading this, took me back to my youth when I sat at a table where my aunt was crying. I later learned that my aunt had delivered a stillborn baby. After reading the books, I learned that back in the day doctors thought if the mother never saw the baby, perhaps she wouldn't feel as though she had really suffered a loss. Obviously that wasn't true!

I would see and hold my baby. I would even have the newborn picture taken to remind me of a soul that is waiting for me in Heaven. The book also suggested having a memento like a ring or necklace. This would help to curb guilty feelings about forgetting our baby over time. Ironically enough, I already had a ring! After a work-related accident, my wedding ring was cut in half. I didn't know what to do with the ring, but after reading about a memento, I knew this was what I was going to use. I now use it as a pinky ring.

Through this experience I learned several unexpected lessons. The one cruel thing I didn't expect is that once you give birth, your body does not recognize whether your baby is dead or alive. It begins the process of preparing your breasts to nurture the child. Every time I felt the milk "let down" I was reminded of something I didn't have. No pamphlet and no person can prepare you for the devastation of those moments. I decided that in order to work through the pain, I would talk about my loss. Each time I shared, the pain subsided more. When we reach out to others in need, our pain becomes smaller. I believe the Lord was able to use this tragedy to cause me to become more compassionate, especially to those mourning any loss.

My greatest desire is for people to know that it is important to not dwell on the "what-could-have-beens" and to be present in the here-and-now. Even when you can't figure out "why," accept that we won't always get an explanation, but the Lord knows the thoughts and plans He has for you.

Getting through the months and even the years to follow were a challenge and at times unbearable. Taking one day at a time proved to be the antidote to that dilemma. I've found that God has taken this painful experience with Elizabeth and has used it to bring comfort to me in other situations.

In 2004, my husband deployed to Iraq and I felt anxious for his safety. While washing dishes, my mind had wandered to Elizabeth and those words, "My grace and strength will see you through." So, I asked the Lord what He wanted me to know because I knew there was a specific reason He brought those words back to me at that time.

God wanted me to know that my future is in His hands. No amount of worrying will make my future more secure. I had to make sure that in EVERY thing I remember that God will see me through.

I'm thankful for the Lord's grace and strength that saw me through. He still reminds me of that often.

Tedianne Toyllens is an Army wife and mother of one who currently resides in Hawaii. She enjoys serving the community through church, military, and school activities. Hobbies include gardening, reading, and bargain shopping.

1 2 Samuel 12:19-20

LIGHTNING LOOPS

By Tashawn Leo

"O Israel, put your hope in the Lord both now and forevermore."[1]

When I was about 9-years-old there was this ride at a popular amusement park called Lighting Loops. I felt excited about conquering this roller coaster, because the year before I was too small to ride. I thought it would be just like the kiddie roller coasters, just a little bit bigger - no sweat!

I soon learned that not all roller coasters are alike.

My big sister and I quickly took the front seat because the front was the best and coolest place to sit. To my young eyes, 45 feet might as well have been 450 feet. The two coasters dived from the platform into an upside down loop that made my brain feel like it was hitting the headrest.

I was crying my eyes out and screaming for my mother, in the agonizing 30 seconds it took to get through the loop and to the end of the track. I knew what would happen next, but there was nothing I could do. I just clawed at the safety bar and waited for that beast to go backwards. I frantically told the operator to stop the ride; I couldn't go back the way I came. I just wanted off that ride and nothing else, but off! Well, that was exactly how I felt, magnified by 100, when my son Sean died.

❧

I was so excited when I learned about his 9-month arrival, but like the roller coaster ride, my excitement was short-lived. We already had one child at home, so I thought, *Hey, we have been through this before and know exactly what to expect.* How wrong we were.

Although our first daughter was born two weeks early, it didn't dawn on my husband and me that something could go wrong with this pregnancy.

So there we were, pregnant again. At the first 8-week check, the doctor said, "Everything looks fine." So of course we were happy parents-to-be.

We arrived at the 12-week check. The doctor said again, "Everything looks fine." He said this although I had lost 20 pounds in 12 weeks and was still dropping weight. I didn't think he was giving me the care I needed. During the same everything-looks-good week, I started spotting. I went to the doctor where they did the usual checks for stress and blood pressure. Then they asked personal questions about my physical activities. The lab investigated any and everything to find out what was going on. Nothing was found, so I went home with the order to take it easy. With a 3-year-old at home that felt impossible, but in the back of my mind I didn't think anything was really wrong because they never found a problem. Here is when my life plunged off its platform, just like on that roller coaster ride.

Although the doctor said everything was fine, I knew in my soul it couldn't be true. The anticipation of riding the coaster was over and the crying for help would soon begin. By the 16th week, I was dilated and the amniotic sac was in the birth canal. Can you guess which part of the roller coaster I was on? I was at the end of my track, crying out to God to save my child.

I was placed in a tilted position. I had to lay with my head pointed down towards the floor and my feet were in the air. It was really scientific. That position should be called the "let's-hope-gravity-does-its-job position." Amazingly it did actually work. The amniotic sac was out of the birth canal. But what goes up, must come down.

That's right, once I was taken out of the position, so was my son. My condition quickly progressed to the point where there was no time to place an emergency cervical cerclage. My platform of relief was gone. So, there we were, terrified, as the roller coaster began to roll backwards.

Over my shoulder I could see the first loop looming, threatening.

By the end of the 16th week, I was very sick from an infection of the exposed amniotic sac. I experienced flu-like symptoms, including a fever, cough, vomiting and I couldn't eat. Once in full labor, there was no stopping the ride. It was just a matter of waiting for Sean to come and go from my arms. At his gestation, I knew there was no way to save him. This was the worse part, waiting for my son to die. I was so, so tired. Tired of praying, tired of putting on a happy face, tired of positive thinking, tired of not crying in front of others. Just tired.

At one point, I thought the nurse put my catheter in wrong because I kept feeling wet. I never thought that it could be my water breaking. I just couldn't believe this was how my pregnancy would end. Since I was sick, I began coughing like I had the flu. I remember trying so hard not to cough, because I didn't want to push the baby out. When I tried to hold the cough in, it came out in forceful explosions of air.

I coughed so hard, the thing I was trying with all my strength not to do - I did anyway. My husband was home attending to our daughter, Theresa, so I called for the nurse. She immediately called him at home so he could be with me. Sure enough, Sean was half way out. She got the doctor right away, but it only took one more little push, and it was over. Then I knew my roller coaster ride had finally come to an end. I listened for the cry of his tiny voice, but there was none.

I felt relieved, yes relieved, because it was all finally over. There was no more guessing about whether labor would stop, no more stress, and no more wishful thinking. There was just no more. My heart and mind finally connected that Sean was gone.

I sat there alone and held my son. He was no longer than an unsharpened pencil, and maybe three pencil widths. I just sat in that bed holding and talking to my son. I told him, his Father in Heaven would take good care of him. I also said that his daddy, mommy and sister loved him very much. I told him we would miss him, but we knew God would be with him always. I held him for 15 minutes, which only seemed like 30 seconds.

Unfortunately, the nurse came and took him away before my husband could get there to see him, too. Our house was a good hour from the hospital. I think it would have been harder for me to let go of him, if I had waited that long. I was so glad, and still am, that I have a husband that supported me through such a time. Just helping with everyday little things like cooking, cleaning, and taking care of our daughter by himself. Plus, he put me first emotionally even though I know he was grieving too. I can never thank him enough for the sacrifices he made.

◌

I call Sean my Blessed Child. If he hadn't come the way he did, his little sister, Mya, wouldn't be here. Through this experience, we discovered I have an incompetent cervix. As the baby gets heavier, my cervix can't support the weight. Complications usually take place anytime in the second trimester.

When Mya came along four months later, the doctors knew what to do to save that pregnancy. At my 16th week with her, I got a cervical cerclage, which is where they stitch your cervix closed. I was still high-risk and sentenced to complete bed rest for the rest of my pregnancy, but that was another roller coaster ride, all its own!

Through these experiences, I learned how to look for God in all situations. There is a reason and season for everything here on earth. I wish I could say, your heart wouldn't ache or you wouldn't have the daydream of what your Heaven-bound baby would look like. But I can tell you, the ache won't sting as much, and there will be a time when you'll smile about having had the opportunity to know and feel your child.

Even in writing this, I got a little misty eyed. However, if this helps one person get through a tragedy, it was worth feeling everything I felt on that day all over again.

Losing my child didn't make me angry. Of course I love Sean and wanted him. But the thing that really lit my fire was how other people reacted to my loss. They didn't know what to say or how to act around me. They avoided talking about their kids or showing pictures, as if it was their fault that Sean died.

My advice? Let yourself cry, let yourself heal, but don't get consumed by the pain. You have to let the grief out and let go of the hurt. You can hold on to the memory of your child, without holding onto the pain of your loss. Let the misery go. As for me, I cried, cried, cried until I couldn't cry anymore. I prayed for healing of my heart and to be strong for Theresa. I didn't want her to see me be a wreck. I also asked God for the strength to go on.

Just because one roller coaster had you gripped by fear and pain, doesn't mean the next one won't make you cry tears of joy. Don't give up your faith. Pray to God and go on your next ride.

Tashawn Leo lives in Fort Lewis, Washington with her husband and two daughters. When not home schooling her children, she is active in her church, Girl Scouts and working toward a B.A. in Education from Pierce College.

1 Psalm 131:3

When Hope
Is Born of Suffering

By Patti Williams

"In my distress I called upon the LORD, and cried unto
my God: he heard my voice out of his temple, and my cry
came before him, even into his ears." [1]

I am sitting in the bathroom while my 16-month-old son, Jayden, splashes in the bathtub. He is beautiful, he is perfect and he is all boy! Jayden is a blessing beyond words because I never thought he would be here.

When I offered to contribute my story, I was unaware that what I had tried so hard to bury would come rushing back to my heart. I write this so I can finish healing my soul and to help other parents find hope in the midst of sorrow.

❧

After 11 years of "not trying," it took several months to get a positive pregnancy test. Finally I had one! It was almost Christmas so I took the pregnancy test and wrapped it and placed it under the tree for my husband, Paul, to open. Having to act normal for a few days was torture because I was practically bursting to tell someone. I was so excited about the pregnancy!

Somehow, I just knew this baby would be a girl so it didn't take long for me to choose her name. We wasted no time telling all our friends and family the good news, and my mother was already buying baby things. Sometime in January we found out Paul was going to deploy for possible war with Iraq. I was beside myself with uncertainty and mixed emotions, not to mention those "wonderful" pregnancy hormones!

I wasn't worried about going through the pregnancy by myself; all of my worries were with my husband and his preparations to leave. As I stepped over his bags sitting in our living room, I tried not to think of the danger that he would be in over there, and tried to concentrate on growing a healthy baby. I was glad he would get to go to a couple of my OB appointments and hear the baby's heartbeat and possibly see the baby on ultrasound before he left. At my first doctor appointment, they took the basic urine pregnancy test, which of course was just as positive at the clinic as it was on my home test. I was definitely smiling now.

Although I was smiling, I felt horrid. My breasts were tender, I felt nauseous and I wanted to sleep all the time. I didn't remember feeling this bad with my first son, Logan, but I attributed this constant flu-like feeling to my being older with this pregnancy. I was definitely feeling every one of my 30 years!

I counted down the days until my first official appointment and Paul had even taken time off from work to be with me. It was February 13 and we were going to go to dinner that evening to celebrate our baby. Paul had been scheduled to leave for Kuwait on February 27 and we had taken every opportunity to be together as a family although our little one wasn't here yet. I was around 15 weeks pregnant.

After vital signs, a Pap smear and what felt like a hundred questions about my last menstrual period, it was time to let daddy hear the heartbeat. The jelly was applied and the doctor put the Doppler machine on my lower abdomen. I have been in the medical profession for over 10 years and I know fetal heart tones are not difficult to find unless the patient has her menstrual dates off and it's too early to hear them.

After about 10 minutes of listening and applying more gel and listening, I began to feel a little uneasy. My pulse began to sprint a little faster when the doctor left to get another doctor to assist her. I kept looking at Paul standing beside the bed and smiling from ear to ear. I tried not to let him see the concern in my face.

A second physician came in and did not try as hard to find the baby's heartbeat, but left to get the portable ultrasound machine.

At this point Paul asks, "Are we going to be able to tell if it's a boy or a girl?"

My heart was racing now as my mind started to search for a mistake in calculations of my conception date. Were my dates off? Did I have a period that I didn't remember? I was almost to the point of being obsessive compulsive about knowing my cycle because we were trying so hard to conceive. I knew I was correct in my calculations.

The ultrasound began and I eagerly watched the screen looking, searching for anything that resembled life. What I saw was a perfectly formed placenta with a healthy, round amniotic sac. That was it.

I strained to see something in there that looked like a fetus, even a very small fetus. After much repositioning and applying even more jelly to my abdomen, I finally saw a very small something.

"So, can you see if it's a boy or a girl?" My smiling husband asked again, blissfully unaware of what was about to happen.

I answered blankly, "There's nothing there." Paul was confused, "What do you mean there's nothing there?" Both doctors were trying to explain things to my husband and I heard words like "implantation" and "endometrial lining" and "spontaneously abort," but I had tuned them out. Inside my heart was breaking. After cleaning up and getting dressed, we left the hospital and drove home. I began to cry somewhere along the way. Paul didn't say anything. I guess he didn't know what to say. The doctor explained everything to us, but I still could not accept it. I had what some doctors call a blighted ovum; others call it a missed abortion.

I had been pregnant, that was definite. But somewhere along the way, probably around 8 weeks, the baby had died. I say "died" because the fetal heart begins to beat around 5 weeks and apparently, around 8 weeks, my baby's heart stopped.

For the next seven weeks my body, having a normal placenta and amniotic sac, kept my uterus in the position to carry a baby. The pregnancy hormones come from the placenta, not the baby, so I continued to have all the symptoms of a healthy pregnancy. The placenta kept growing and so did the sac, however the baby had slowly diminished. Usually this type of condition will abort itself early in the pregnancy but because I carried mine for 15 weeks, I thought it an even crueler act of nature.

The next few days were horrible and I wanted a D&C. My physician said it may actually scar my uterus and prevent me from having another pregnancy so she didn't do them.

Eventually my body would figure out I was not carrying a viable fetus and it would abort on its own. Basically, I would miscarry via nature. I was upset because I had the remains of a baby inside me and I wanted it out of my body. If I could just not be pregnant anymore, then all the hurt would go away. Or so I thought.

I tried to remember everything I had eaten or drank that might have caused this to happen. Did I cause too much stress to the baby because I was so worried about Paul leaving for Kuwait? One thing was clear, no matter what had gone wrong; it was my fault.

It took seven days, many tears and many trips to the bathroom before I started spotting and then the spotting turned into heavy bleeding. Seven days after that, I stood in the middle of a cold helicopter hangar in the middle of the night and said goodbye, perhaps for the last time, to my husband as he left on a C-130 airplane bound for Iraq, and for war. Before he boarded the plane I told him I was sorry I'd lost his baby. I had lost my child and my husband within two weeks.

∽

I can't describe the loneliness I felt. It was deeper than anything I had ever experienced before. I had wanted this baby out of my body and now that it was happening, I wanted to keep it inside for just a few more days, so I could say goodbye. My ex-husband and his wife had welcomed a healthy baby boy into their lives at the end of January and although I was happy for them, I couldn't help, but feel envious. As a matter of fact, I was envious of any pregnant woman I saw. Maybe envy is not the right word. I wasn't really jealous, it just magnified my overwhelming sadness. I was miserable. I didn't get out of bed for about three days. I felt so physically sick from the miscarriage and emotionally, I had no husband to hold me and tell me it was going to be alright.

I had heard every comforting word in the book and some not so comforting words. People said things like, "You'll have more children,"

"Maybe it's nature's way of getting rid of the babies who have something wrong with them," "You can try again," and "It just wasn't meant to be."

My loved ones didn't realize that I didn't want to have more children, I wanted that child. I don't want to have a baby to replace that one. I wanted her! I was angry, but I didn't have anyone to be angry at.

I never blamed God for what happened, but I will admit that I questioned Him. Why me? Why now? Why did He even allow me to get pregnant if He was going to take the baby from me? What was I supposed to learn from this? Why? Why? Why?

One day I found myself in the middle of my living room floor crying out to God. I cried, yelled and prayed, hoping for some answer to why this had happened to us, to me. I read the Bible out loud, which is something I never do, I just didn't know who else to talk to. At least hearing my own voice reassured me that I was still alive. I read:

"In my distress I called upon the LORD, and cried unto my God: he heard my voice out of his temple, and my cry came before him, even into his ears," Psalm 18:6.

"I will cry unto God most high; unto God that performeth all things for me," Psalm 57:2.

And lastly, A Psalm of David: *"Unto thee will I cry, O LORD my rock; be not silent to me: lest, if thou be silent to me, I become like them that go down into the pit. Hear the voice of my supplications, when I cry unto thee, when I lift up my hands toward thy holy oracle,"* Psalm 28:1-2.

The answer never came. The answer still has not come. I know one day it will be told to me. But it will be in God's way and in His time.

❧

By mid-March, I couldn't stand to be in this house by myself anymore. Watching the news of the bombings in Iraq was making me crazy. I packed up a suitcase and went home to Florida. I got my old job back working for a physician in a family practice office and I tried to put it behind me.

Nine long months later, my husband came home from Iraq for his two week mid-tour break. As luck would have it, I was ovulating when he came home and I found out I was pregnant shortly after he returned to the Middle East.

I was even more excited than the first time. God had given me a second chance! I told everyone I knew that I was pregnant and began to take even better care of my body than before. Six weeks into this pregnancy I began to bleed at work. One of our female physicians examined me and didn't see anything irregular with my cervix and told me that sometimes women spot during the first trimester and it's perfectly normal.

Just to be safe, I saw an obstetrician nearby and my worst fears were confirmed. It was happening again. An ultrasound revealed that this baby was very small and that either my menstruation dates were off, which I knew they were not, or this baby was in trouble.

I was told that the baby was either dying or already dead. No heartbeat was heard. I was crushed. And again I was without my husband to support me. Once again, I was going through a loss all by myself.

Because Paul was stationed in Mosul, Iraq, telephones were not an option and he was literally living in the trenches. He got to use a computer about once a week and I had to tell him through an e-mail that I had lost his baby, again.

I felt pain, but this time it was worse than the first. There was a physical pain, but I am sure it was caused by my aching heart. What did I do to deserve this? Why was God doing this to me? Was I being punished for something I did? Just someone help me and tell me what to do to make this hurt go away!

I had lost two babies in a row. I had barely had enough time to heal from the first blow and wham! Here's another one.

All the doctors had told me that the odds were with me carrying this baby to term. One miscarriage is not uncommon, but two in a row does not usually happen. Grief overwhelmed me. Once again, I had to tell friends, family and Logan that I had been pregnant, but wasn't anymore. I went through every scenario trying to think of something I did to cause the miscarriage.

My hormone levels were normal and even my Pap smear had been good. The only explanation the physician could come up with was that the lining of my uterus, where the egg attaches itself and begins to grow, was not rich enough in nourishment to sustain life.

Maybe it was my age. Maybe it was stress. Maybe I was working too hard. Maybe it was the stress of having a spouse in a combat zone. I just wanted an explanation. Anything. I was adopted when I was three-weeks-old and I adore my parents. Adoption was not out of the question, but on the Army's salary, we knew it was probably impossible to afford it.

When my husband returned from Iraq in January of 2004, we decided to try one last time. If this pregnancy didn't take, then he was going to have a vasectomy. In April of 2004 I had my first positive pregnancy test. Immediately I went to the doctor to confirm the results.

Every week, I had hCG quantitative testing done and to my surprise, the numbers doubled just as they were supposed to. Paul and I decided not to tell anyone about this pregnancy, including Logan, until we were at least through the first trimester. Seventeen weeks later we were elated to tell the world! We were so excited and were glad that we were finally able to share our joy. To say I was overcautious with my body is an understatement. I was so scared that I would lose the baby that I don't think I began to relax and enjoy the pregnancy until about the 28th week!

Jayden Paul Williams was born January 6, 2005 at a healthy 8 lbs 6 oz. Although he was not breathing well on his own for the first five hours, each passing day he improved. We brought him home four days later. He has grown and blossomed into his own little being and I adore him.

&

I know there are other moms and dads who have endured greater tragedy than I have. Maybe you have had a stillborn baby or an infant death soon after birth. Maybe the problem is not being able to get pregnant at all. My heart aches for you.

In everything there is a blessing even though we might not see it. God sees it. In time, we will see our little angels again because they are waiting for us in Heaven. There is a reason that God gave us these babies, no matter how short their time. They were a part of our lives and always will be. I will hold each one of these previous pregnancies dear to my heart because Jayden's birth was not a replacement of them; he was an addition to them.

Each loss is preparing us to become the person God wants us to be. Each loss is a learning experience even when that lesson is so hard that it breaks our heart. You and I were chosen to be the mother or father of that special baby at that special place in time.

I still deal with guilt from time to time, especially when what would have been my due date passes by. But I have come to realize that pain is a natural way to heal. Without the hurt there is no healing. And I still have a long way to go. Be strong, beloved, and always remember that you are never alone.

Patti Drake Williams is the mother of two boys, Logan, 11, and Jayden, 16 months. She and her husband, Paul, are currently stationed at Ft. Campbell, Kentucky, assigned to the Army's 101st Airborne Division. In 2007, she will graduate from Austin Peay State University with a degree in secondary education.

1 Psalm 18:6

WALK THE WALK

By Aprill Williams

"Beloved, think it not strange concerning the fiery trial
which is to try you, as though some strange thing happened
unto you: But rejoice, inasmuch as ye are partakers of
Christ's sufferings; that, when his glory shall be revealed, ye
may be glad also with exceeding joy." [1]

As a Minister of Music I never thought I would have to deal with such things as infant loss, depression, or anger and frustration with God. I thought for a while I would skate by because I was doing God's work. I shouldn't have to go through what others went through. I was under enough stress, just trying to live right and do God's will.

I should never get so comfortable with God that I feel exempt from pain, hard trials or tribulations. I had a first-hand experience with this matter when after waiting four years to have another child, the unthinkable happened.

It was the middle of the night in 2003 when I woke up to use the bathroom and discovered I was bleeding as though I were having a menstrual cycle. I was 10 weeks pregnant.

I immediately told my husband and we agreed he should stay home with our two sons who were sleeping. I called a girlfriend to come and take me to the emergency room.

The ER doctor sent me home with a diagnosis of a threatening miscarriage. He said to follow up with my OB/GYN the following day and return to the ER if the bleeding soaked four or more pads within an hour.

Upon following up with my OB/GYN, she told me my baby was not developing and was measuring only five weeks. They checked my hCG levels and asked that I come back in a week to get them checked again and to have another vaginal ultrasound. They told me if the levels were consistently getting lower and if the baby had not developed anymore, they would have to terminate the pregnancy.

I went home that night, fell down on my knees, and prayed. I knew I was not strong enough to allow them to terminate my pregnancy. So I asked God to spare me the agony of waiting a week to know our baby's fate. If it was His will, I wanted God to allow me to miscarry. I couldn't make the decision to terminate my baby's life! What if there was a possibility the doctor was wrong? I just cried out to God.

Well, God heard my prayer. Five days later, I attended church on Sunday, went to the altar, lifted my hands and gave my child back to God. I had already begun excessive bleeding and clotting that morning so I knew what was happening. I had to go to church so that I would be able to accept it. Almost immediately after the prayer, I was literally on the floor with severe cramps. For a few minutes, that's all I remember. After regaining my composure, I asked one of my friends to rush me to the emergency room because I could tell the bleeding was soaking through my pad.

I felt emotionally drained, but didn't cry at the hospital because it was too late; I knew my baby was gone.

ᴏ

After sitting in the lobby for what seemed like eternity, I was finally brought back to a room. When the doctor tried to do a vaginal exam, something blocked her view. She removed what seemed to be an extremely large clot and placed it in a specimen cup on the counter, directly in my line of sight. I could only think of my precious baby lying in that cup.

Again, the ER doctor told me to follow up with my OB/GYN the next day. I did as she instructed and found that my normal doctor was unavailable and I would have to see someone else.

This is when I was treated as if having a miscarriage was a daily occurrence for me. The resident doctor was very dismissive and not sensitive to my feelings or physical well-being. After I explained the problems that occurred over the weekend, she did an abdominal exam and told me I could get dressed. I pleaded with her to do a vaginal ultrasound to make sure everything was okay.

She rudely responded to my plea, "If they said you miscarried at the emergency room then you miscarried."

"Well if you don't mind I would really like to know that everything is gone," I repeated.

"I really don't think it is necessary, Mrs. Williams."

"Well I do! Could you get another doctor please?"

"I'll be right back," the resident said with a huff.

I overheard a supervising doctor tell this young lady that she needs to follow the patient's request and give the appropriate care. She also told her if she was not there to actually witness the miscarriage then she could never be too sure that all the tissue was removed.

Despite the supervisor's rebuke, this experience left me feeling stressed and depressed. I could not imagine experiencing anything like this again. Both the treatment by the medical staff and the loss of my baby had a profound impact on me. I tried to mask my feelings. I was in denial about the whole situation for a long time and didn't want to talk about it. I have always been perceived as being strong and having a tough exterior. I tried to keep up this façade. I tried to block it out of my mind, but it still bothered me.

Instead of trusting in God, I decided to take matters into my own hands. Although I had two handsome sons, and still wanted to try for a baby girl, six months later I tried to end the emotional pain by having the Essure Implants[2] placed. They are the equivalent of having one's tubes tied. For me, this was a permanent solution to a temporary problem.

❧

My husband didn't show or express his emotions. Neither did I.

We put up such a front that it was believable for a while. I made up several excuses and even threw God in them.

I said, "He knew what He was doing when this happened," "He knew this would be a financial burden," and other ridiculous excuses.

I reasoned why the surgery was a good decision. Only recently did we admit that we did want to try for a girl. I believe my husband knew how badly I was hurting the whole time. This is why he agreed to the Essure Implants. He sacrificed his own wishes so that I wouldn't have to suffer anymore. I wish he had known that my suffering really only began once we made that decision. Thankfully, it didn't affect our intimacy. We just tried to ignore what happened and worked on our feelings individually.

I now know that getting those implants in my tubes was the biggest mistake I could have ever made. Although, in making this mistake, I lost faith in what God can do; He still grants His mercy on me everyday. He is a forgiving God.

Eventually, I was able to grow closer to God and forgive myself. I realized I wasn't hurting as a result of the miscarriage anymore. My pain stemmed from the decision I made to stop believing that God could bring me through anything! I wanted to just be numb, unable to feel that heart-wrenching pain again.

Since then, I've grown closer to God and am able to understand His Word a little better. When faced with future tough decisions, I can trust Him and not create my own drastic solutions.

If a situation is brought upon me, I can handle it. He isn't going to put more on me than I can bear. As a singer, I was able to take the lyrics to some of the songs I sing, apply them to my life and for the first time in a long time – walk the walk.

A favored scripture says, *"What is it then? I will pray with the spirit, and I will pray with the understanding also: I will sing with the spirit, and I will sing with the understanding also."*[3]

✆

Too often we fall to our knees praying to God for answers or help after we are faced with adversities. When we learn to praise God through, and in spite of our circumstances, we will find that life is a little bit easier to deal with.

We must have an understanding that in our walk with Christ, we will have hard trials and tribulations. This is inevitable. It is our relationship with God and our faith that helps us to get through those hard times.

We have to seek His face daily - then our lives can be made whole. Cast your cares on Him. Believe that He will do what He says. He cannot lie nor fail.

My prayer is that someone, if only one person, be touched by my story and will begin to truly seek God's face and His will for their lives. The loss of your baby does not have to mean the loss of your life, sanity or faith. Allow God to make you whole as He has done for me.

Aprill Williams is married to an Army nurse and is the mother of two boys, ages 9 and 7. She sings in the choir, is the praise team leader, and a member of the praise dance team. She lives in Whitehouse, TX.

You can reach her at aprill_w@cox.net.

---

1 Peter 4:12-13

2 Coiled implants placed in the fallopian tubes that permanently block the egg from dropping into the uterus.

3 1 Corinthians 14:15

Part Three

A TIME TO HEAL

Always Mother

By Carlton L. Gillis, Sr.

*This is the gift, the greatest of all, the gift that cannot be
shaken
No matter the cost you may count as lost, motherhood
can never be taken*

*T'was God Himself who breathed this endowment, to
last this life and beyond
What power or brood or circumstantial mood, can
destroy this eternal bond?*

*Wind forces, divorces, intimidating noises, even visiting
yours at the tomb
When God says it's done, then life has begun, because of
who came from your womb*

*Your womb was ordained, so motherhood reigned, t'was
not just a feeling or wish
The table was set with the knife and the fork, the spoon,
the cup and the dish*

*Is not a chair still a chair, when no one sits there? I say
yes tho' it sits all alone
The same with a mother, who sits alone waiting, when
that child's not coming back home*

So when's a good time to stop being a mother, never be
motherly again?
Never! No, never! I say it again; someone else needs that
kind of friend

What God put in you, was not a mistake, nor "this
thing" that you're dealing with
The command to honor your mother rings true, look it
up, you'll find it's the fifth

So mother you were, mother you are, and mother you'll
always be
Christopher 1, Kasimir 2, Elyana 3, they're just in
safekeeping you see

So these are the words I have for YOU, 'cause you will be
one way or another
'Till God gives your own, or that others have sown,
remember you are always Mother.

Faith After You're Gone

By Barbie Schmidt

"To know her is to love her; and once you love her, being apart from her is unbearable." [1]

My 2-year-old daughter, Sarah Faith, stood in the doorway of my bedroom with arms crossed and gave a stomp of her little foot. Her head tilted down and her Precious Moments eyes looked up. She was upset with her 11-year-old sister, Leslie, for taking a pen from her. Apparently she wasn't finished with the masterpiece she was creating on her leg. With a big sigh, Sarah looked at Leslie and cried, "Meany!"

This would be the last word we ever heard her say, and June 28, 2005 would become the day that changed our lives forever.

We had two safety gates set up in the living room. One at the top of the stairs leading to the front door and lower level of the house; the other across the kitchen doorway that gave access to the sliding glass door and back yard. I was constantly making sure the gates were shut so I was surprised when I saw the one at the stairs standing open.

Sarah liked going downstairs because some of the older kids' bedrooms are down there, so I had Leslie see if Sarah was with her 13-year-old sister, Chelsea. They both quickly reported that Sarah wasn't down there anywhere. This is when fear took over. I was suddenly frantic. As a rule, Sarah couldn't open the front door and I knew I hadn't heard it open or shut. Where could she have gone so quickly? When your child manages to disappear you don't really think rationally.

Someone said "Oh my God!" I'm not sure who. It even could have been me, I just remember hearing it. Leslie went through the kitchen, to find that although the safety gate had been closed, the latch wasn't secured. As

I went into the back yard, I heard a scream. The sound was indescribable and the most terrifying noise I ever heard.

I don't remember going around the side of the house to the swimming pool. I just remember seeing Leslie rise up out of the water with Sarah in her arms. She quickly handed Sarah to me as Chelsea came through the sliding glass door. I screamed to Chelsea to call 911.

I immediately flipped Sarah over so that I was carrying her face down. I ran up the stairs of the deck and into the house, repeatedly pumping her abdomen. Water poured from her mouth. When I got inside, Chelsea was on the phone with a 911 operator. I laid Sarah on the floor, put a rolled towel under her neck and began CPR.

Sarah was pasty white and her once bright, sparkling blue eyes, were empty and gray. Each time I gave her a breath, I had to turn her head and clear water and foam from her mouth. I was nearly hysterical, screaming for God to help me, to make her breathe - just one breath - PLEASE!

Chelsea handed me the phone so the 911 operator could instruct me. I was frantically working to get Sarah to breathe and already doing everything the operator told me to do. I don't know what I said, but the next thing I knew, the lady asked if there was someone else she could talk to. I yelled "NO!" into the phone and threw it down. By then, I heard the sirens as the ambulance came toward my house. I continued pumping, counting and breathing until the paramedics pulled me away. Within seconds my house was full of medical personnel and police officers.

An officer whisked my girls downstairs. They were in shock and terrified. All they could do was stand in horror as they watched me try to bring Sarah back. Another officer pulled me into the kitchen. I grabbed the phone to call my husband, Steve, at work and tell him what happened. The officer started asking questions, but I couldn't answer; I couldn't put a sentence together. He asked if there was someone else he could call for me. I rattled off my mom's number and he called and told her there had been an accident and to come right away. She only lives a few blocks away and could get here quickly.

I tried to get into the living room to see Sarah, but the officer was persistent about keeping me in the kitchen. I could hear the paramedics talking, but there were so many, their voices all ran together. Finally one of them shouted, "I've got a rhythm!"

Just as they took Sarah to the ambulance, my mother, niece, nephew and Steve all showed up. We decided that me and my mother would follow the ambulance and Steve would stay with the kids and answer the questions that I was unable to answer for the police.

Before I knew it, we were pulling into the parking lot of the ER where a paramedic was waiting to take us in through the ambulatory entrance. Steve's dad, Johnny, and my step dad, Ron, were already there; Sarah was in a room with the curtains closed. They gave me a chair outside the room while we waited. We have six children and half of them weren't present. We needed everyone there because if the worst happened, they had to be able to say goodbye.

My mind raced with images of Sarah. Sarah running and playing, laughing and singing, then Sarah limp in my arms. How did this happen? It's just not possible. This beautiful, perfect child was now fighting for her life. In my 33 years, I had suffered a first trimester miscarriage, a second trimester miscarriage, the death of family members, friends and even a counselor. I thought I knew pain. I had seen death stare me in the face as a boyfriend looked into my eyes and took his last breath when cancer took his life. I now felt a pain I never knew existed; a fear that knows no words. I couldn't think nor could I breathe; I wanted to see my baby. I wanted to hear her call out, "Mo-mmy!" Just like at home when she would wake each day. How was it possible that something so horrible happened so fast?

Oh, Sarah. Determined, independent Sarah. She felt so comfortable in the water. I had taken her to swimming lessons at the YMCA before we purchased the pool. She loved the pool and just thought she could do it by herself. She was too smart for her own good. We had created so many memories; she was so amazing to watch. She loved to play peek-a-boo and we'd chase each other through the house. She loved books and her family. She loved Sponge Bob, Care Bears, snowmen (they were all "Frossy" to her) and she *loved* her Fuzzy Bunny (a floppy purple bunny she got for her first Easter), it went with her everywhere. Much like the Velveteen Rabbit, it has been well loved and shows it. She loved people, she loved God and she loved to sing and dance. I'd watched her memorize songs on the radio in the car and sing along with her siblings. I was in awe of her everyday. At naptime each day she watched a video of "Psalty Little Praisers" (she just called it "Salty"), a children's Christian character. Her favorite song was on this video, "Say to the Lord, I Love You." Sarah quickly learned the music and sometimes changed the tempo and made it sound more hip-hop. Never before had I known a child at such an early age to know the Lord as she did. I loved the way she said *Jesus* when she sang "Jesus Loves Me," when she brought me her angel bear that sang it or pointed Him out in her Bible story books. She could never push the button in the bear's tummy hard enough, so she would bring it to me and just say 'Jesus.' Would I ever experience these things again? Would I ever hear her voice or her laughter, her little feet running through the house? Would I hear her squeal when we played peek-a-boo around the side of the couch or hear her cry whether it was for me or out of anger at me? Would I watch her grow up? Would "meany" be the last word I would ever hear her say? Please God, no! I needed to hear her say, "Mommy, I love you!"

✑

I snapped out of this random collage of memories and thoughts when the doctor came out. They had revived Sarah, but she had a collapsed lung and wasn't yet stabilized. While they tried to stabilize her enough to relocate to PICU, they moved us to a waiting room where we would have some privacy. Steve and his mom, Karen, arrived shortly after, along with numerous other family and church family members who came to show support and offer comfort and prayer. After what seemed like hours, the doctor came in and asked everyone to step out of the room.

All I could do was cry; I can't remember ever feeling so afraid of anything in my life. He told us that Sarah was as stable as possible, it looked grave and chances of survival were very slim. By the time she was resuscitated, Sarah had been without oxygen for nearly 30 minutes. He was preparing us for the worst. I remember very little about the next couple of hours.

✑

Sarah was now stable, but still on life support and had not regained consciousness. We could see her, but only for 5 minutes every 15 minutes and only two visitors at a time. It was a jolt to see her lying there hooked up with tubes and monitors. She felt so cold and looked pale. She had to be warmed slowly so I resisted my maternal instinct to cover her. I couldn't take it all in, it seemed utterly impossible that my gorgeous, charismatic, lively, happy child was lying there lifeless. How could God let this happen? I kept wondering where He was when my precious child was slipping away. I felt He had abandoned us and sat by doing nothing while I fought to save her on that living room floor. The God I knew would never take such a wonderful child from us, would He?

This is the kind of thing you hear about on the news. It doesn't happen to you and not to your child; but this time it did happen to us and it was our child on the news. As the hours passed, many visitors came and went. Many people prayed at the hospital and others began 24-hour prayer chains. People around the globe were praying for our precious daughter, from here to Iraq and back. It was a touching and moving show of support.

By this time two of our children, Brandon and Donovan, made it to the hospital, but our daughter, Lenae, didn't arrive until later. My dad, Paul, also arrived from Oklahoma. Chelsea and Leslie stayed by my side. Leslie had been in her wet clothes for hours when a nurse finally offered her scrubs to wear and dried her wet clothes. Steve, the kids and I were all holding onto each other as if our lives depended on it. That night all the kids left with their grandparents and the nurses gave us a parent's room to sleep in during Sarah's stay. We didn't sleep. We couldn't sleep! If we did, we would miss our 5 minutes with Sarah four times an hour. It seemed horribly cruel. We wanted to be with her every second and waiting was so hard. Knowing that we could do nothing to help her was difficult to accept. I'm the mommy; I'm supposed to be able to kiss the "ouchies" away. I wanted to kiss it away more than anything in the world.

We spent our time with her, telling her that we love her, kissing her little cheek and forehead and holding her tiny hand. I wanted desperately for her to squeeze my hand back, but she never did. The first night was uneventful and torturous at the same time.

○

The second morning, the doctor had good news. Sarah's lungs, heart, kidneys and other vital organs had healed a great deal during the night. He was amazed by the improvement. The healing was happening almost too quickly and he cautioned us not to read too much into it. I felt hope for the first time since the accident. Throughout the day, we spent more time with Sarah and took turns hanging out in her room. We even got her the "Psalty Little Praisers" video to play in her room and tucked Fuzzy Bunny under her arm. We repeatedly played those songs, hoping for a reaction. Many visitors brought gifts of food, prayer and companionship. We had to lean on each other and make sure our family was going to be okay, no matter the outcome. Sarah would want that. I couldn't breath.

Although Sarah's pupils were responsive for the first time, a neurological exam showed no mid or upper level brain activity. Only stem and lower level activity was found. This was crushing news. If her brain didn't recover, Sarah would live this way the rest of her life. She probably would never wake up, be able to do anything for herself or be active again. The doctor also said to be prepared for what may happen when the swelling started. Sarah's whole body, including her organs, would swell, likely causing more problems. It felt like a roller coaster ride. We got bad news then good news then more bad news. We didn't know how to feel.

Later that evening, we hurried into PICU and saw nurses and doctors furiously scurrying and the doctor barked orders and reprimands all at the same time. We stood outside the room watching as we held onto each other. We were terrified that we had seen Sarah alive for the last time.

Later we learned that a change in her chart had been missed, so Sarah coded after being given the wrong medication. Also, she was very critical and was not to be left alone under any circumstances. This order wasn't followed, either. A recliner was moved into her room and we stayed with Sarah for a while. Later, Steve tried to sleep and I stayed with Sarah and rested in the recliner. Although her machines alarmed all night, I held her hand, laid with her, hugged and kissed her, talked to her, prayed for her and cried for her. I couldn't bear the idea of losing her, it was too awful to even consider. I had to believe that she was going to be okay. God was going to perform a miracle!

On day three, another problem was discovered. Sarah's other lung had collapsed during resuscitation after the code. The machines alarming during the night should have alerted the nurse of a problem, but he didn't detect anything wrong. Sarah was not doing well.

As the prayers continued, we pushed on, hoping for good news. A second neurological exam showed no improvement in brain activity and her pupils were no longer responsive to light.

During this time, I was beginning to crack after more than 48 hours of almost no sleep. I'm scattered on the details, but so much happened so fast and there was so much in and out with everybody, we never really sat down and told the kids how grim Sarah's situation was. We gave them only the information they needed to know.

Steve wanted me to rest a while and said he would get me if anything changed. Less than 30 minutes later, Steve arrived with the nurse. Things had taken a turn for the worse. Sarah's vitals dropped and it was growing more difficult to sustain her life. We had to make a decision. I went numb. This had to be a dream, Sarah had to be okay! Steve and I sat in that dark room crying in each others arms looking for answers we didn't have. She didn't have much time left.

We called everyone who wanted to be there, to be by her side. There were about 20 to 30 people in Sarah's room, so everyone could hear everything that happened next. Even with a crowd of supporters, I don't know that there was any comfort anywhere. I was just devastated. All I know is that all those people loved Sarah and I didn't want to take this opportunity away from anyone who wanted to be there to say goodbye.

The doctor cleared the room of everyone but Steve and me. He needed to know what to do. The doctor said we were no longer prolonging life, but that we were only prolonging death. Sarah was going to die no matter what they did. We could keep her on life support until she passed or we could remove her from the machines allowing her to pass in the arms of those who love her. We hesitantly chose the latter.

The tubes and IVs were removed. The nurse wrapped Sarah in a blanket and Steve picked her up. He held her, kissed her and told her he loved her then laid Sarah in my arms. We sang her favorite song and her siblings and grandparents held her one last time.

In the weeks prior, my step dad and Sarah had grown very close and he couldn't bear to say "goodbye," so he left the room. Her grandparents kissed and held Sarah close. Of our children, Leslie seemed to have the hardest time at the end. She ran from the room and no one could find her for several minutes. Like my step dad, she just couldn't say goodbye, but during her moments away, had a change of heart and returned.

There was such calm in the room and although there was so much sadness and we all cried, it felt like the room was filled with her spirit. Instead of going hysterical, I just felt *her* and as hard as it was to say "goodbye," I knew she was okay. I could feel her fill me up. I just felt her. As I held Sarah, we said a last prayer and at 3:42 p.m., the doctor pronounced her dead.

We then had the opportunity to parent Sarah one last time. We bathed her, changed her diaper, dressed her and I fixed her beautiful blond hair. I held Sarah until Steve said we had to go; she had begun to stiffen. I couldn't absorb what had happened. It was too much to wrap my brain around. Leaving the hospital without Sarah was the hardest thing I have or will ever have to do. I felt as though I was abandoning her. I remember telling the nurse to keep her wrapped in the blanket and making her promise to stay there with Sarah Faith until the coroner came to get her. I couldn't stand the thought of her being there alone, even in death.

Our family was completely traumatized. How are children supposed to deal with seeing their beloved baby sister as she lay dying in front of them? We were broken. I literally felt my heart tearing in two. How could we leave without our sweet Sarah-bear? This wasn't right, something was horribly wrong. This was not how it was supposed to turn out! NO, NO, NO, NO, NO!

In the following days, we all wrote letters to Sarah; which were read at her funeral. More than 200 people attended and witnessed the balloon release. In the eight months since we lost our Sarah-bear, our family has suffered deeply. We spent Thanksgiving back in PICU after two of our children overdosed on medication during the night; they wanted to go be with Sarah. One child had to spend a week in a mental facility afterward.

We've dealt with severe depression and anxiety requiring counseling, psychiatric help and medication and I had another miscarriage. All this added to our grief.

Each of the children was given one of Sarah's stuffed toys to keep and sleep with at night. They have found some comfort in this. Steve and I kept Fuzzy Bunny. Sarah was never without it and in her memory I continue to take it everywhere I go and I sleep with it each night, just as she did. I too have found comfort in it.

The sadness in our home is ever present because a large part of our life is now missing. We have attended a grief group for those dealing with the loss of a loved one. They can understand our pain. We prayed so hard for what we wanted, forgetting that we were supposed to pray for God's will. God allowed us the glorious privilege of being her family, knowing and loving her. What a wonderful, beautiful gift He gave us, but in the end she was meant for Him.

Through my pain I have experienced the power of prayer. I now know that God never left us, He was there the entire time, holding Sarah Faith in His gentle, loving arms. Those first weeks are now a blur of sorrow, pain, tears, disbelief, anger and severe longing to have her back in my arms, which continues today. We may live the rest of our lives with broken hearts, but I know the Lord will sustain us.

Sarah *Faith* Schmidt. Her name was no accident and this is her legacy. It is because of Sarah that I have a deeper, truer love of God and a faith unlike any I've ever known. With a newfound faith, prayer, love, support of family and friends and the many memories of Sarah etched in our hearts; I know we will get through this, together.

Barbie Schmidt lives and works in Wichita, Kansas. She is a proud wife and the mother of six beautiful children. She spends her days taking care of the house and taxiing kids to and fro. She can also be found at the cemetery or visiting Sarah's memorial Web site at www. sarahfaithourangel.memory-of.com, keeping her memory alive.

1 Barbie Schmidt

No Rain, No Rainbow

By Tania Marble

"The one thing I do know is that through everything, with patience and with love, is hope."[1]

There's an old saying, "no rain, no rainbow." In my life that has meant, I have had to go through horrible and at times painful experiences before things made sense and blessings came.

My drizzle turned into a torrential downpour before I was 24 years old, but eventually, I have been able to see the rainbow in my own sky. To be blunt, I'm not sure how in the world it happened. Five years have passed since the rain began, but just three months ago I finally learned to see the blessings in my life.

In January 2006 , I decided to visit my best friend in Hawaii. Since my husband, Brian, was in Iraq for the second time with the 101st Airborne Division, I figured I'd have a little fun and relieve some "deployment stress" by tanning on a beach. At first, I was a little hesitant to go because my friend just had a baby the previous year, and I would be there for her daughter's first birthday.

I felt nervous being there because I already had so much pain and aching in my heart for a baby. I didn't know if I could handle being around a baby for two weeks without feeling a little resentment. Once I saw that smiling little belle, somehow, I knew that everything was going to be alright.

☙

As a little girl, all I wanted to be was a stay-at-home mom when I grew up. I had friends who wanted many great and ambitious careers, but I was the one who wanted to marry the man of my dreams, buy the cute little "all American house" and have a family. Some said it was because of my strong Latter Day Saints up bringing, but I wanted to achieve my goal because I always wanted to be like my mom, my hero.

Well, things started out according to my plan. I met the man of my dreams; we fell in love and married in June of 2001. We became pregnant right away. I thought I had everything figured out. When we miscarried five weeks later, people said it was "normal" and not to be too alarmed. I was crushed, but I tried to listen to those who said it was "normal" to miscarry once or twice before a healthy pregnancy. It was nice hearing comforting words, but half the time, I really wanted everyone standing there with babies to just go home, and I hoped their babies stayed up all night crying extra loud!

My plans fell to pieces on September 11, 2001, as it did for many others. The events of September 11th sparked fervor in Brian to join the military. So a couple of months later, after I was getting over miscarriage No. 2, and some other medical issues, Brian joined the Army as a Blackhawk helicopter mechanic. I was pregnant again, but just after he left for training, I miscarried. Not having Brian there was the hardest thing. Knowing I had lost yet another baby made me feel lonely enough, but to have my husband gone for a seven-month stretch made it all the worse.

After Brian completed basic and advanced training, we received orders to move to Fort Campbell, Kentucky. Sad, but true, I had to look on a map to see where the heck Kentucky was. It is actually a beautiful place, so when we arrived, we bought a cute little house and I became pregnant with our fourth baby. Five and a half weeks later, that pregnancy also ended in heartache.

I had become a desperate woman. Desperate because when I married Brian, he said he wanted eight kids. That's how many kids were in his family, and he loved having a big family. To me, every time I lost another baby, I felt more and more like I failed Brian. I felt less and less like a woman and more like a burden to my husband. He, of course, was wonderful to me. He always knew the right things to say and do. But then he was gone. His new unit headed to Iraq. Just like that, my support, my friend, and my lover was gone for a year.

Now, I consider the time Brian was in Iraq the first time as my "irritated as hell" period. This was a "fun" time in my life where random people from social or church functions would give me their take on why I wasn't carrying to full-term and what they thought I was doing wrong. Well, seeing how my parents tried very hard to raise me with some manners, I would usually just sit there and smile and humor whomever I was talking to, and then walk away, at times muttering choice words under my breath. Sometimes I would say that we might want to adopt later down the road after Brian applies to officer candidate school or makes a higher enlisted rank.

On one occasion, someone said it was selfish of Brian and me to put his career before having kids. My absolute "favorite" part of this period was when one woman had the audacity to say I wasn't a worthy woman and that my husband shouldn't be with me because I couldn't give him children. Oh, how that comment haunted me.

One doctor thought that if I were to lose weight, hopefully my hormone levels would be high enough early on to sustain a successful pregnancy. I opted for gastric bypass surgery since losing weight has always been a struggle even after diet plans, personal trainers, and diet pills. It all went fairly smoothly. I had an excellent surgeon and I bounced back pretty quickly. From my highest weight to my lowest, I lost 120 pounds. I thought surely now I could be fit enough to have a baby, right? Yeah? No.

Brian came home from Iraq the next winter. This started the "confused as hell" period of life for me. I had yet another miscarriage, and yet another doctor told me what went wrong this time. I can remember thinking this couldn't be my life. I was supposed to be the stay-at-home mom driving my little girl to ballet and soccer practice. My husband was going into a civilian medical career when we married, and now he was a war veteran in Kentucky, of all places!

I did everything the doctors had asked. I even just about sawed my body in half to lose weight in hopes of carrying full-term, and it still wasn't happening. I was getting angrier at myself and at God for how everything was turning out. At the same time, everyone else seemed to be having babies all around me. Even the freakin' dog next door had a litter of puppies! I knew I hit bottom when I looked at a pile of newborn puppies and was actually jealous of the mama dog's ability to give birth to all seven puppies. That wasn't a good day for me.

At the same time, my best friend told me she was pregnant. I tried really hard to be happy for her. I tried to be supportive. But part of me felt jealous and slightly resentful. Here I was hurting and aching for a baby, and she made it seem so easy. It just didn't seem fair. I love her like a sister, hell; she's closer to me than most sisters are to each other. Then she dropped the other bombshell. They were moving to Hawaii.

Alright, now God must REALLY hate me, right?

The event that really marked the closing of one door and the opening of a new one was when I lost a set of twins. It was my sixth and last pregnancy. That same day, I had an ultrasound to see if everything was alright with the pregnancy. Since I was extremely high-risk, the doctor wanted an ultrasound very early in the pregnancy. It confirmed I was carrying twins. Oh, I was elated!

My husband is a twin, and it has always been our greatest desire to have a set of twins, too. I couldn't wait to tell Brian. I even made him a cute mini-paper bag scrapbook telling him all about our little twins. It was my dorky creative way of telling him the good news. Well, three days later, the miscarriage started, and my dream ended.

By the time I got home from the hospital, Brian's unit had already thrown his butt on a helicopter to fly him back to Kentucky from an air gunnery range in Illinois. I didn't think they would fly him home for something like that, but his unit was very supportive and knew of our previous losses. They made it a priority to have Brian by my side.

Later that night, Brian's supervisor and his wife came over with flowers and dinner for us. They were so kind and told Brian that if we needed anything at all, to call on them or anyone else at the unit. They will never know how much that simple act has affected my life. With our best friends and family on the West Coast or in Hawaii, they did what very few others did or could do. They didn't say much on the topic. They didn't offer crazy advice that doctors haven't already talked to us about. They were just there and listened. Yeah, bringing a hormonal girl fried chicken was also a big hit, but they started the healing process for me. For that, they will always be in my prayers.

I honestly thought I was doing alright with my grief from our losses, but when Brian's twin brother called later that summer to say his wife was pregnant and her due date was my birthday, holy flaming Moses, did I feel the pressure then! I was now the only married woman in Brian's family to not have kids. Everything people had said during the past four years was stirred up again. Oh, Brian could not have left at a worse time. He left in September 2005 for another year in Iraq.

I was in Hawaii the night things really clicked in my heart. My best friend and I stayed up really late and just talked. You know, it was one of those really great girly talks where you end up crying, hugging, laughing, all the while downing a bag of mint Oreo's and some Diet Coke. I think it's funny, eating Oreo's with Diet Coke, as if the Diet Coke is supposed to balance out the Oreo's!

Anyway, that night she told me to be happy with who I am. That God has a plan for me. God wouldn't give me more than I could handle. She said I should embrace my youth and be content with the idea of not rushing adoption; to let things happen when they will. She reminded me that I had seven babies in heaven, so if I adopted even one child, Brian would have his eight kids, and I would have my one. So in a very odd and crazy way, God would have been looking out for both of our desires. She went on to remind me that I did marry at a young age and that waiting until I am 30 to have kids isn't going to be the end of my world.

The laughing portion started when she reminded me that I could still have sex in the middle of the day, but that would soon stop when we had kids. On that night in Hawaii the rain stopped and the sun began to shine in my life.

One week later, Brian was home for, I guess you could call it, his "two weeks vacation from war." We stayed in Seattle for a week with my family and spent a week in Salt Lake City with his family.

As we drove back to Seattle from Salt Lake City at 3 a.m., Brian's twin brother called from the hospital to say his wife just gave birth to their son. Something inside told me to turn around and surprise them at the hospital. So we did.

My rainbow appeared for the first time as I held my newborn nephew that early winter morning. What a sweet spirit filled that room as mother, father, and son bonded. Seeing Brian hold his twin's infant was such a joy to behold. I knew from that moment on that everything was going to be alright.

❧

Everyone has a rainbow in their lives. Sometimes it's just hidden by a few clouds. Some are hidden in a drizzle, and others go through a torrential downpour. I'm not sure why some people seem to go through more trials than others. The one thing I do know is that through everything, with patience and with love, is hope.

Before Brian left to rejoin his unit in Iraq, he said a few things that sealed the deal for my rainbow's permanent place in my life. He said we would be parents someday, but until then, he was just happy to have me in his life. We both mourn the loss of the babies we could have had. We often think of the family that could have been. How old our children would be today, what they would look like, the things we could have done together.

The thing that has helped me get through a lot of the grief was realizing that losing our babies wasn't my fault. It wasn't planned; it just happened. I can still accomplish my dream of being a stay-at-home mom, but we have now decided to wait a few years before we adopt a child. The irony is I really am going to be like my hero, my mom. My brothers and I are adopted, too.

Tania Marble is a supportive Army wife, originally from Woodinville, Washington and is currently stationed at Fort Campbell, Kentucky with husband, Brian. Tania enjoys various things ranging from traveling to cooking, but most of all, she values precious time with her husband and family.

1 Tania Marble

A PAINFUL GIFT

By Jamie Hart

"What we have once enjoyed we can never lose
... All that we love deeply becomes a part of us."[1]

I remember the screams and tears I cried when I was told my child was gone. Before I could even blink, my fairytale life was crushed and torn. I was forever changed by a battle I never expected to fight - a mother's grief.

The first time I saw that precious, growing body on ultrasound, I became a real woman. My child was conceived in love, and each day he grew inside me, that love intensified. I have so many memories of the time spent with my baby boy. I remember the daily expectations of feeling the first movement and later being overjoyed, and often annoyed, with the "constant jazzercise" going on in my womb. Our secret talks were so special. I loved singing to my baby as he swayed to my lullabies. I remember how my heart raced the day the nurses searched for a heartbeat, and I'll forever be haunted by the doctor's words:

"There's no easy way to tell you this, but there's no heartbeat."

☙

All of my doctor visits were routine, but the baby looked very big and my blood pressure was elevated at the last two appointments, so at 37 weeks the doctor stripped my membranes and prepared me for an induction. After the procedure, I began having mildly painful contractions. By the next day, I knew I would be having my son soon.

Family members rushed to finish up the nursery and I ran around like a triathlete, still in pain. Usually, the baby's movement overwhelmed me, but when someone brought it to my attention that I hadn't been complaining; I didn't give it a second thought. I had been on the go since dawn and didn't have time to pay attention to movement.

After finishing up the nursery, I showered and went to the hospital triage with my mother. I never thought something could happen that would change my life for the worse.

෨

When I arrived, I put on the dreadful hospital gown and waited for the doctor. Nurses hooked me up to the usual monitors and searched for a heartbeat using the Doppler. When she couldn't find one, she summoned for the doctor. This time the doctor checked for a heartbeat using the ultrasound machine. His face was emotionless, but his eyes stared with desperation at the screen. It was then I knew that my first and only child was gone. His words announcing my son's demise burnt my eardrum as they seemed to take over my body like a ripple effect on a once placid lake. Immediately, I screamed my son's name.

"Miller!" I yelled. I shook uncontrollably and got out of bed, walking back and forth, as I screamed. The cries echoed in the once serene hospital hallway.

I decided to stay and give birth to Miller, so a nurse wheeled me to a room that stood far away from the rooms where "happy mommies" gave birth.

I was given strong doses of medication to settle me down and numb my horrific pain. My family was there, holding my hand in absolute shock. When I was given an epidural my water broke and it was full of bright, velvety blood.

After a medicated sleep, I woke up to the doctor's voice followed by the reality of this nightmare. For nine months, I'd developed such a great relationship with my doctor. We were always joking and making crude comments about being pregnant. This time his face wasn't lit up and his eyes didn't beam like usual. I asked him to give me Versed[2] so that I wouldn't have to experience the actual delivery. In fact, I begged. No way would I watch my miracle enter this world so silently. I couldn't bear to put any more energy into this pregnancy, it was over and my baby was dead.

Miller Neely Hart was born still at 6 lbs 14 oz and 20 ¼ inches long, on January 23, 2005 at 7:34 a.m. I awoke to the sounds of my family and the doctor sobbing. The room was so still, just like my son. A nurse swaddled my precious child with a blanket and delicately placed him in my arms. He had such angelic features and his body wasn't warm, but not yet cold. I wanted to wake up and look into my baby's eyes but instead I was forced to hold a lifeless gift in my arms. I did my best to look Miller over, still dazed. As I held his perfect little hand, I prayed that he'd wrap his newborn fingers around mine. I kissed Miller's now cold forehead while his father sobbed. My tears ran down our angel's face as my body shook like an earthquake.

His soft, newborn smell will live with me forever.

❦

From what I remember, my father planned a lovely funeral. My mom led me into the funeral home and into the room where I would see Miller for the last time on earth. Knees shaking and extremely fatigued, I knelt down before an angel. Family members had gently tucked pictures, notes, teddy bears and blankets into his white casket. I wanted to pick up my son so much and don't know why I didn't, other than feeling like it wasn't an option. Looking back, I realize it was something I should have done.

In the days after the funeral, I was hospitalized again and diagnosed with Post Traumatic Stress Disorder. Doctors grew puzzled by my uncontrolled crying and violent shaking. They also expressed frustration because I refused to speak to someone who hadn't lost a child of their own. By the grace of God, someone introduced me to a dear stranger who is now a lifelong friend. Suzanne lost her sweet son to a heart defect at five-months-old, so she came to wipe my tears away. My new friend encouraged me to keep a journal and be open about my thoughts. She said ALL the right things and comforted me in ways that my own mother couldn't do. I thank God for her daily. Her help inspired me to reach out to others facing this type off loss and I highly recommend others doing the same.

I wrote Miller a letter describing my true feelings. The words seemed to bleed onto the page from my pen. I wrote:

Sweet Child,

I never got to hear you cry, see you smile, or tickle your feet. But I'll dream about it and pray that we'll meet again and embrace each other. Please forgive Mama for doubting God, for feeling jealous of others, for shutting out people who care. I'll never stop loving you or remembering the happiness I felt with you inside me. Please listen to my silent prayers for you, my silent promises, and the songs I sing to you. I was born to be your mother – whether you were born dead or alive. You were born to receive my love and we must believe together that we can still communicate with our hearts. I will love you forever.

After Miller died, my pain wasn't only emotional. It grew physical. My soul was forever changed. I felt battered and broken. My son was the light that opened my eyes and gave me sight - now I was alone in a dark place. I felt bruised and shaken, ripped and torn. I kept my jaw tightly clenched, as if my teeth were wired shut, in order to cause a nauseating pain. To numb the pain, I turned to alcohol. Not even Suzanne knew how much I drank. When I mixed booze with the strong prescription medications, I lost all ambition. What was left of me slowly died. I was a time bomb, the living dead, living to die. I can't remember when it got bad, but it turned ugly quickly.

Two days before Miller's first birthday, while drunk and confused, I decided to attempt suicide by overdose. I drove to the Christmas Box Angel statue at a local cemetery and lay there, motionless. If not for a desperate call to another dear friend, who also suffered the loss of her infant son, I would have succeeded. It was there, as the emergency crew tried to save my life, when I realized I didn't want it to be this way. Yes, my grief was severe and strong, but this wasn't the honorable way. Dying this way wouldn't make my angel proud and if I were gone, who would be here to remember him?

I rehabilitated myself through church and Alcoholics Anonymous, and am sober now. I also sat down with my family and confessed my addiction and that I didn't want to do it anymore. When I discovered I couldn't hold on to my pain, it was a life-changing moment that will stick with me forever. I believe my son is with God and I am comfortable with that. Without the support of my parents and close, dear friends and; without a renewed faith in God, I don't know where I'd be.

༄

On Miller's first birthday we had a small celebration. With a few close friends and immediate family, we had cake, sang "Happy Birthday," and opened a gift. It was a happy day without tears. I released more than 30 decorated balloons in hopes that they would reach Heaven. When the same hands that longed for Miller to wrap his delicate, newborn fingers around them, let the balloons go – I also let go of the hatred. I accepted what had happened to me and despite my pain, I saw a future. I moved on with my pain and truly dealt with it. I opened up doors for others in their grief, buried myself in books of child loss and sorrow, and learned how God would be my guide. After all, He lost His only son, too.

I believe that I was given Miller as a gift but his time was short. He was baptized in my love as I carried him in my womb. Every tear I cried reinforced my love and continues to give me hope that I will see him again. I AM A MOTHER and that can never be taken away from me. Nothing can stop me from loving Miller and keeping his memory alive. I honestly believe that my child lives through my eyes, and in that, I feel it's my purpose to live a happy life for us both.

I still cry now and then, the holidays are no easier, and each month when the 23rd comes around my heart fills with suffocating love for my child on his angel date. For healing, I continue to write in my journal and send messages to my son in Heaven. But, sadness and grief will not overcome me, nor dictate my life. Whether God blesses me with another child or not, I feel I am a strong mother and I have a child who is safe in "perfection." After all, the only thing I ever wanted was to give Miller everything and to put the world in his hands.

He has that now, so I am at peace.

Jamie Hart lives in Pensacola, FL where she works with children and continues to raise awareness for pregnancy and infant loss, as well as helping other bereaved families. You can reach her at hewasstillborn@aol.com.

1 Helen Keller
2 General anesthetic

Born Too Soon

By Samone M. Starnes

"My soul is weary with sorrow; strengthen me according
to your word."[1]

Imagine my surprise when the test showed a positive result! We were going to have a baby! I didn't think it would happen because I have endometriosis[2]. Also, during my last pregnancy, I was diagnosed with an incompetent cervix, which was a double whammy!

Several days after finding out I was pregnant, I began spotting. The doctor did an ultrasound and we were able to see the baby. I felt so much relief when he said he didn't see 'active' bleeding. He recommended progesterone injections, to help strengthen my uterus so I started the injections that day.

Each week, I visited the doctor faithfully and got an ultrasound to ensure all was going well with the baby. I was the happiest that I had been in a long time and also the sickest.

I suffered terribly from morning sickness. Everything made me nauseous, yet I had to eat for my baby. The doctor prescribed some medications, but they didn't seem to work very well. I finally had to use a medication given to chemotherapy patients. I continued to suffer from nausea, vomiting, and indigestion. I took Maalox often, so my mother began calling the baby "Maalox;" a nickname that stuck!

I was approximately 9 weeks along when I started feeling pressure in my lower abdomen. I thought it was kind of strange that I would feel so much heaviness so soon in the pregnancy. I had reason for my concern because my last child was born prematurely, at 25 weeks gestation.

The doctors told me any future pregnancies would require a cerclage and a C-section.

I'm a soldier in the Army and am usually seen at a military facility. My "high risk" status meant I was supposed to see a specialist at a civilian hospital, but somehow the referral was not processed for several weeks. By the time I was scheduled for an appointment, I would have been 19 weeks when I should have been seen between 14-16 weeks in order to get the cerclage.

∞

No section leader wantd me on their team because I was pregnant. Their big question was, "What if you go into labor early?" If that happened, the section would be forced to carry my workload. I felt driven to show everyone I was just as capable and competent although I was pregnant. I had early days and some late evenings, not getting off until 5:30 or 6 p.m., at times.

In retrospect, I may have pushed myself too hard.

On Sunday, March 12, 2006 I awoke to a popping sensation and fluid coming out of me. I jumped out of bed, scared and shouted, "Oh my God, my water broke!" I ran into the bathroom, where I emptied my bladder, but fluid continued to gush out of me. I stayed on the toilet until it stopped. I told my husband, Johnathan, I needed to get to the hospital. He quickly dressed and I thought this could not be real. My bag of waters could not have ruptured; it was no where near time for this to be happening! I was in shock.

We arrived at the hospital, but the medical clerk at the front desk did not grasp the gravity of the situation. After checking me in, she instructed me to have a seat and a nurse would be with me. I felt angry and frustrated. Did this clerk not understand what was happening to me? I wanted to grab her and force her to get someone to take care of me, but I had to remain calm. I was already scared to death; I didn't want to make things worse.

By this time, more fluid started gushing out, but there was nothing I could do. I was out of my mind with worry! What was happening to my baby? Why was this happening to my baby? I eventually made it into one of the exam rooms, and at that time I asked my husband to call my mother. Shortly after, a nurse came in with a Doppler to check for my baby's heart tones. Her heartbeat sounded really strong which was a relief to me! The doctor arrived and referred me to the civilian facility.

After an ambulance ride to the other hospital, I hardly settled into another exam room before a doctor did a vaginal exam, took cultures, did an ultrasound and explained what was happening.

There are several possible outcomes of not having any fluid around the baby. Without any amniotic fluid, my baby was not protected from getting an infection, nor was I. If the pregnancy did continue, my baby could be born with various health problems.

We were left with a couple of decisions; we could let them induce labor and end the pregnancy or we could wait and see if some fluid would re-accumulate around the baby. The chances of the latter happening were less than 10 percent. We were given some time to decide.

I told Johnathan I did not want them to induce labor. I wanted to give our baby a chance although I knew her chances were slim. I just couldn't end her life, though. She had such a strong heartbeat. I knew that if I rested, I would be able to carry my baby until the point where she would have had a fighting chance. Just knowing there was this little life growing within and depending on me, filled me with joy. I imagined who she would look like; whether she would take after me or her father. Despite the endless morning sickness, complications and everything; I desperately wanted my baby.

No one was able to tell me why my water broke and I did not have an infection. I was admitted into the hospital for 48 hours of antibiotics and then released with instructions to follow up with my doctor in one week.

Strict bed rest and a prescription for a thermometer; that was the treatment plan. I did not feel comfortable leaving the hospital, but the doctors were supposed to know what was best. I wondered how I could do strict bed rest when I knew I'd have to get up to use the bathroom.

At home, I carefully followed doctor's orders. On Friday, March 17, an ultrasound revealed there was a little fluid around the baby's head. He said there was also probably fluid behind the baby, which he couldn't see. She still had a strong heartbeat and I had not dilated. He told me to continue doing what I was doing and to continue praying.

I felt so optimistic on the way home. I just knew that if I continued on bed rest, I would be able to get my baby to the point where she was considered viable!

It was a little after 8 p.m. that evening when I went to the bathroom. As I started to wipe myself, my hand got caught on something. I looked down and saw my umbilical cord hanging down. Fear enveloped me! Why was my cord hanging down? I stayed in the bed, like I was supposed to, except to use the bathroom. What was going to happen to my baby? I knew what having a prolapsed cord meant, but I didn't want to accept it; I couldn't accept it. I got off the toilet and told my husband to take me to the hospital. He called my mother en route.

I was taken to an exam room right away. Two nurses were unable to find my baby's heartbeat, but they said not to worry. The doctor confirmed that I had a prolapsed cord and I was transferred to the civilian facility.

The doctor examined me and asked if I wanted an epidural. I remember lying there, wishing that it was just a bad dream. I was almost 19 weeks, this could not be happening! I was supposed to see the specialist in a few days and fluid had re-accumulated around the baby's head. I had felt so much hope.

A nurse started some IV fluid, and eventually the anesthesiologist started the epidural. I believe the doctor may have gone somewhere to take a nap because I did not see her for several hours. When I did see her, the following day, she did another vaginal exam, and told me to push. When nothing happened, she left and returned around one hour later with the same instructions.

The next time she came into the room, she did the same thing, except this time, she told the two nurses to grab my legs and push them back. My mother held me, while my husband was on the other side of the curtain. The doctor told me to push, but this time I felt emptiness.

I asked my mother if my baby had come out. She said yes and I started screaming and crying. I had never known a pain like the pain I felt right then. It was not a physical pain; it felt like my soul had been torn out.

After the nurse had cleaned our baby up and placed a pink dress on her, Johnathan held our baby girl. There was so much sadness in his eyes. His first child, our dream, would not be recognized. He held her so tenderly and looked at her with so much love.

Later, I asked Johnathan, why he had stayed on the other side of the curtain. He told me he couldn't bear to see our child born dead. He wasn't sure how he would react; whether he would pass out, run out the room screaming, or hit someone.

My baby was gone at 18-5/7 weeks. My baby girl, who I had watched grow from a little speck into a little human. Even though I could not feel her every movement, I saw her bouncing around during the many ultrasounds. What happened to the baby I saw trying to flip over? The baby that was so full of life? How could she be gone?

When I first learned about our pregnancy, I said I would name a baby girl after me. When the nurse asked our baby's name, my husband told her Samone Monique, after me.

If it were not for the fact that she was born so tiny, one would not have known she had been delivered straight into God's hands; she looked like a sleeping angel. Samone Monique was so very beautiful and so small; she weighed only 7 ounces. Her ears had not completely moved into position on her head and she had no hair, but she was one of the most beautiful babies I had ever seen.

Samone had a tiny face with the most perfect little nose. She also had these cute little lips, with the lower lip looking as if she was pouting. She had long, slender fingers with long fingernails; it was almost as if she'd had a manicure. Her legs were tucked under her and I was afraid to take them out from under her. My mother, who held her a little later, did untuck her legs to see her feet. My mother told me Samone had long toenails, as well.

When I held my baby, I talked to her. I told her how much I loved her and how much I had wanted her. I told her about her brothers and sisters, who had been looking forward to meeting her. While I held Samone, I wondered why she was taken from me. From the time I found out I was pregnant until I delivered, I did everything I was supposed to do.

I went for prenatal care; I never missed an appointment. I took the progesterone injections for several weeks. Why was I being punished? Nothing could possibly hurt more than losing my child. It felt as if my heart had been ripped out.

☙

A little later, my mom went to pick up my four children who wanted to see their sister. My children gave me hugs and kisses. They also brought balloons and this statue of God's hand holding a baby with angel wings; I started crying again. Each child held their sister. While my oldest daughter held Samone, she could not stop the tears from flowing.

My oldest son cried so hard his body shook. Everything in me wanted to stop the hurt and take the pain away. As parents, that is part of our job, but I was helpless. After a few minutes, my mother handed Samone to my youngest daughter. My baby boy scooted next to his sisters so he could see "Maalox." He then held her while my mother made sure he would not drop her.

After everyone had said hello to their sister, my mother suggested I let the nurse take Samone so that she would not be "out" too long. I did not want to let my baby go. When the nurse came in, she told me I could keep Samone with me as long as I wanted. Could she stay with me forever? I knew I could not take her home although God knows I wanted to.

My mother asked if I wanted a memorial service for Samone. I had not even thought about that and didn't want to think about it. Did I want to have Samone cremated? All I wanted was my baby; I did not want to have to deal with these options! I should not have had to deal with this kind of decision! The nurse gave my husband the information about the funeral home and he tended to the details of her cremation because I had some unexpected complications.

I stayed in the hospital for eight days and needed two D&C procedures. On day six of my hospital stay, I was placed in the hallway after an ultrasound, where I heard someone having their baby's heartbeat monitored. I could not take it, I began crying. I felt like I was losing my mind!

By this time, Samone had been cremated. The day she was cremated my husband brought me a beautiful frame that had "Baby Maalox and Mommie" engraved on it. He also gave me a silver box that matched the frame.

The nurse who had been taking care of me when I delivered Samone gave us a bear wearing the dress that Samone had worn, along with the blanket she was wrapped in; a certificate, and a small version of the New Testament (with Psalm and Proverbs), in which she placed our daughter's footprints.

My husband also brought Samone's urn to the hospital. When I looked at the small urn, a feeling I cannot fully explain overwhelmed me. I couldn't breathe. My precious baby was inside of this tiny container! Everything seemed so unreal. I was still hoping everything was just a horrible dream although I knew it wasn't.

I still remember when I first heard Samone's heartbeat. I remember when she first started forming the little buds, which would transform into her arms and legs. I remember when she first began to look like a little human being.

She was an active baby. I remember watching her movements during the many ultrasounds. She would turn over as if she was disturbed by the doctor scanning my abdomen. One day the doctor pointed out how Samone was opening and closing her mouth, taking in the amniotic fluid. It seems unbelievable that an active, growing baby could be gone.

❦

My husband and I went to a grief counselor, who referred us to a group in our area that deals with infant loss. I have gone to see a psychologist because I thought I was losing my mind. I still feel that way. It has been one month since my baby's death and I still do not know how to deal with it. I am still angry with God and have been told that it was His will, but how does that help me?

I am too scared to even think about having another baby for fear that the same thing will happen again. I believe Samone was probably my last chance to have another baby. I try to put on a brave front, but on the inside, I am dying. There is so much emptiness inside of me, left by the loss of my angel.

To console me, people have reminded me that I still have four beautiful children. I agree and am very grateful for each of them. I love my children with all of me, but I still have suffered an enormous loss. I lost my baby. No one should have to endure such a tragedy.

All that is physically left of my daughter is the teddy bear, ultrasound pictures and the few pictures a kind nurse took that day. I have Samone's urn, which sits on my nightstand next to her framed picture and the matching box.

I pray one day I will be able to think about Samone and smile, knowing that she is being well looked after and that I will see my baby again. Until then, I hold onto the memories of carrying her in my womb, holding her in my arms, and seeing an angel who was born too soon.

Samone M. Starnes is an active duty member in the Army. She is married to another servicemember and has five children; three girls and two boys. They currently reside in Augusta, Georgia.

1 *Psalm 119:28 (NIV)*
2 *A condition where tissue typically found inside the uterus is found inside the abdomen, on the ovaries, ligaments that support the uterus and other places. The disease causes painful lesions and bleeding outside the uterus during the menstrual cycle.*

Until We Meet Again

By Wendy Bartolini

"I thank my God upon every remembrance of you."[1]

I couldn't believe it. I just wanted to die. I didn't know anyone who had gone though this and didn't know what to think, do or say. I instantly dreaded going home, thinking of all the baby things I had already received. All the e-mail newsletters I signed up for and the daily questions. How was I going to make it through the next day?

It was October 28 at 10 a.m. and I had a regularly scheduled 24-week appointment. My husband, Manny, always tried to go with me but I told him it was not a big deal and to just go to work. Besides, he was a helicopter pilot and had a flight physical scheduled that day.

Earlier, I felt concerned because I wasn't feeling the baby move much. But that morning my husband and I both thought we felt something. What we must have felt was just the beginning of heartache.

∽

Typical of a regular appointment, they listened to the heartbeat with a Doppler. The nurse couldn't find it. She assured me that sometimes the baby just gets in an odd spot and it is hard to find.

Nonetheless, the doctor immediately sent me for an ultrasound. It felt like an eternity, but really was only a minute until the technician told me "I'm so sorry but there is no heartbeat." I thought my life was over. I sobbed uncontrollably and almost felt like I was going to faint any minute. What did I do to cause this? We had just moved and I thought our baby's death was my fault because I had been too busy. I was outside in the heat during a garage sale; did that do it? Was it the stress I felt after the Army told us we might be moving to Korea?

141

I met with the doctor who instantly told me they would induce labor that evening. The doctor also called my husband and told him what happened. I was in no condition to talk. Manny immediately came to the hospital and we both sobbed in each others' arms. We were then told to come back at 5 p.m. to start the induction. I didn't want to go home; I didn't want to go to Wal-Mart.

I was so afraid to see another pregnant woman, to walk near the baby section, to see a newborn. I just wanted to curl up and die. We ended up going to our storage facility to pay a bill and the lady at the front desk asked me when I was due. It was just the start of a very long road.

We returned to the hospital and continued the nightmare. The doctor offered me any medication I wanted for the physical pain, but none of it helped to ease the burning in my heart. Even though I was out of it, I remember telling my husband I thought I was going to die - or was it that I wished I would die?

My mom and sisters flew from California to be with us. We needed the support. My husband and I talked about whether we would hold our son, Lincoln, and he was sure he would. I, on the other hand, didn't think I could do it. I thought it would be too emotionally hard. I couldn't imagine the pain.

However, when Lincoln was born I knew I couldn't let him go without holding him. He fit in the palm of my hand. The nurses put a little blue hat on his head and wrapped him in a blanket. It was amazing and a moment I will never forget. He looked just like Manny. My husband also held Lincoln and I felt even sadder watching the two of them together.

Would Manny ever get to hold another baby of ours? Would this happen to us again? Would he resent me for not being able to carry a baby? We had no idea what the future would hold for us as parents.

In the days that followed, we cried all day. My husband took time away from work so we could focus on each other. The cards and flowers came and we tried to make it through each day. The hardest thing was answering other people's questions. Everyone wanted to know details. People said the worst things to try to console us.

I will never forget when someone said, "Maybe God wanted you to have a girl."

The most common comment was, "You will have another baby." At this point who knew if that was true and who cared? Every single one of my friends got pregnant that month of our loss and I couldn't bear to talk about it or share in their joy.

I wanted my baby Lincoln who had just died. Nobody seemed to understand. My relationships with God and my husband grew during this time. We started praying to just make it another day. We also found a couple that had been through a loss at 23 weeks and they were a huge help to us.

We finally found someone that understood each thought and every tear. To avoid feeling hurt, I began to exclude myself from events of pregnant friends. I had to protect myself and start my healing process. After a few months, I was able to go out, but still came home in tears.

My husband was a captain and we were stationed at Fort Rucker, Alabama, but we wanted Lincoln buried in California where we grew up. We had a small funeral there with family and close friends. A childhood friend did the service where we played the song "Glory Baby," which moved everyone to tears. It was a gloomy, rainy day we will never forget. The weather even played off of our feelings.

We wondered once again how we could go on. I wrote this letter in memory of our son, Lincoln Aleksander Bartolini:

To Our Dear Son Lincoln,

Please take these gifts: Mommy's baby blanket to comfort you; Daddy's bearcat to keep you company; a guitar pick for all the beauty and music you represent; an American flag so you will always have something of which to be proud; and a note to remind you of how much we love you. We cannot wait to hold you again in Heaven.

We miss you already and love you infinity,

Mommy and Daddy

Here I sit almost three and a half years later and, surprisingly, the pain is a lot less. I will never forget Lincoln nor will the pain ever fully go away, but I can say it is less. I started to focus on telling my story and helping others that had gone through a loss. It was the main way I have felt some sort of relief. After Lincoln's birth, we discovered that I had several medical conditions that caused our loss. I had to learn that the things I did during my pregnancy did not cause his death. Deep down, I knew that already, but felt I had to put the blame somewhere.

We started a tradition on the first anniversary of Lincoln's birth. We gather the number of balloons that match the age he would have been, then write a poem and attach it to the balloons. Before we let the balloons go, we say a wish to Lincoln. The first year I cried non-stop and hated our new tradition. The second and third year I felt rejuvenated. I also read online what others have gone through and joined a support network. I learned to focus on the end result. Lincoln is in Heaven and one day we will be there with him as a complete family.

Since our loss we have had another son, Jaxson, who is 23 months. He is our miracle baby. Doctors said the possibility of having children was slim but with prayer and determination, we have been blessed. I also suffered two more miscarriages and am currently 23 weeks pregnant and on bed rest with another baby.

I dream of the day when we'll get to meet all our babies in Heaven and spend eternity with them. We have God watching over us and lots of guardian angels to protect us. The pain does get better, but there will always be a place in my heart for Lincoln and the two babies we lost through miscarriages.

Wendy Bartolini is a stay-at-home mom to Jaxson, 23 months, and is expecting another son, Carter. She and husband, Manny, reside in West Chester, Ohio with their dachshund, Tamale, and Chihuahua, Jobu.

1 Philippians 1:3

Dan Dan

By Abigale Peszeki

"It's so strange how hard I fell for you although I just met you. Now I miss you and long for the day when I'll hold you in my arms again."[1]

My 2-year-old son, Danny, slept quietly in the next room. For the first time in four months he was feeling better. He was able to push himself up, he could eat without a tube and his lungs were clearer. I gave him a breathing treatment and the vibration from the machine made him wake up with a protest.

That's my strong little boy, I thought.

I could tell he had his fight back in him. I picked him up, all 35 pounds of him, and sat him on my lap. His curly blond hair was messy and his cheeks were lined and red from sleep. He turned his face up to me and snuggled under my chin. A chubby hand patted my arm. I squeezed him tight and kissed him, thanking God for his sudden recovery.

Later that day, Danny became restless, and wanted to be held. He wanted me to sit with him, so I left the laundry in the washing machine and sat with him on the couch. I sang all his favorite country and pop songs. He would drift off, and then wake up to check if I was still with him. He grunted for me if I got up and walked away from him. I loved these times, when we would just lay together and enjoy each others' company. It always felt like our struggle wasn't so bad when we had each other. I knew he loved me, and I loved him, and nothing was in vain.

Danny died the next day.

꩜

Things weren't always so hard. My husband, Balázs, and I were married in Iowa and a couple weeks later we moved to his hometown in Gődőllo, Hungary to start our life together. Our healthy son was born two months later on February 4, 2001 in Budapest. The next three weeks were tough, as they always are with a new baby. But it was wonderful getting to know his personality and establishing a routine.

He isn't pretty, I thought, *but he is so cute!*

I felt more love for him than I ever knew I had in me. Like a lot of new parents, I had plenty to learn about this new little person in my life, and I wanted to be the best parent I could be, and give him all the things I never had. One day, I held him on my lap and gazed into his big blue eyes, and he stared back at me. He made little faces, and had a look of wonder on his face. He had a little cone head covered in blond hair, a dimpled chin, and the softest, almost musical voice, and he was red-faced. What I didn't know was that Danny was harboring tiny bacteria that would destroy him and turn our lives upside down.

One morning, when he was three-weeks-old, we woke up to find Danny crying and very sick with a 104 degrees fever. We rushed him to the hospital but it was four hours before someone told us what was wrong with our son. The doctor spoke Hungarian to Balázs about what they found. Although I didn't speak Hungarian, I knew right away when he pointed to the neck and back, that Danny had meningitis. I felt my knees buckle, yet I didn't feel the full impact of the situation at that point. I didn't cry. I didn't know how to react. I never saw this coming, because our son was healthy and normal in the beginning. Balázs stood facing the window. He had tears in his eyes and voice as he translated what the doctor said to him.

"He said he has meningitis and that he is in critical condition," Balázs relayed. It hit me only after I heard those words in English. Our baby's life was in danger.

Four hours after we arrived at the hospital we were allowed to see our son. As we walked into the room, I was hit with an indescribable pain when I saw Danny attached to a ventilator and tubes. His eyes were covered, and his body tightened up during seizures. He was unresponsive to our voices. I couldn't hold him and could do nothing to protect him.

I felt I had let him down in a very big way, and that feeling is something I can't begin to describe. I experienced mental and physical pain when I saw my child suffer. All I could do was stand by and hope that the people caring for Danny were doing everything possible to save him.

That night neither of us slept; we took turns at his side. We watched the monitors and felt anxious every time something beeped. The weeks after our son fell ill were a blur. While in the hospital for a month, I pumped breast milk every two hours and hoped this would be over and he would recover soon. I went through the motions, pumping, trying to eat, and leaving my son's side only to use the bathroom or shower. I could not believe this was happening to us, I felt angry, confused and extremely helpless. How could I not have seen this coming? Why me? Why us? What in the world did I do or not do to bring this on? I knew life, as we knew it, was over. We had just turned down a long and painful road.

After four weeks, I started going home at night. It was very hard to kiss Danny goodbye. I always expected him to be awake and looking for me when I came back the next morning, but he never was. Our lives were a living nightmare and although stress was high, we stayed strong for our son.

❍

I hated everything about the hospital. This was a Hungarian hospital, stuck in the dark ages. It was filthy and cold, without hot water or toilet paper in the restrooms. People stole from one another and I wasn't used to the culture. I felt stupid for having ever come to Hungary to give birth in the first place. Our son was extremely sick. I knew this because the doctors showed Danny to their colleagues like they were studying him. They would shake their heads and talk amongst themselves. Sometimes, they would say *anyukaja*, which means "his mother," and I knew they were talking about me. I felt horribly depressed and lost. It seemed like everyone at the hospital looked down on me as a parent, at least I looked at myself that way, so I assumed everyone else did, too. We were told our son's recovery was unlikely, and when I heard that the first time I wanted to jump out the window.

One day while doctors examined him, Danny pulled the tube to the ventilator out of his nose and began breathing perfectly. Surely this was a sign he is getting stronger, we thought. The doctors were amazed. He never needed the machine again. Two weeks later, we were able to hold, hug and even breastfeed him. He hadn't lost his ability to eat. This alone was a miracle. Since Danny wasn't infection-free, he stayed in the hospital. He also needed several tests and ultrasounds to determine how much damage had been done. He also occasionally needed to have fluid drained from his brain chambers because of edema[2].

Just before Danny's discharge, three and a half months after he was first hospitalized, the head doctor sympathetically explained that our son would never recover, because of severe brain damage. Danny was deaf and blind. He slept all the time and his speech had been affected too, which explained why he didn't cry.

"Danny, will not live very long," the doctor explained. "He has very slim chances, if any, of recovering. It would be a miracle if he survives to the end of this year."

This was painful to hear, but I felt my son's age would give him more of a fighting chance. We would prove the doctors wrong. I had become extremely bitter and hateful towards the doctors and hospitals in Hungary, even though I knew they were right, someone had to take the blame for his condition. I didn't care what they said. We had been praying hard for Danny's recovery. I was confident that he would eventually heal, then wake up and smile at me one day. We were sent to another hospital for two weeks to evaluate just how severe the brain damage was before Danny could go home.

At the next hospital, we were only allowed 30 minutes every three hours to be with Danny and feed him because of the tests and therapy. Going into the room to feed him, I would see his little hand stretched out looking for me, and my hopes lifted that just maybe the therapy was going to help him to develop and recover. I held him, smelled his hair and kissed him over and over. By this time, he was gaining a lot of weight and the nurses would comment that he was eating too much. But in reality, the hormones in his brain were not well regulated, which made him prone to obesity. At the end of those two weeks the doctor in charge informed us that therapy for Danny would be a waste of time.

"*Anyuka*, he doesn't even know who you are. We cannot do anything for him here, but you can find therapy for him for your own peace of mind. You will not have much time to be with him," she said with a sort of smirk on her face.

She then advised that because we were so young, and able to have more children, we should put Danny in an institution. As we went home that day, I thought about what she said. Yes, our baby was broken. No, we would never send him anywhere, and yes, he does know who I am. He might be broken and disabled but he is ours and we will fight for his life.

If I could point out one thing that hurt my self-esteem the most, it's that my son was considered "retarded" as a result of his illness. I hate that word, and would never have used it to describe him because Danny was as much a person as anyone else. In the hospital, the doctors would use that word, and I would cringe every time I heard it because there was a time in my life when I thought "retarded" people were scary. When I was younger, I used to feel sorry for the parents of disabled children and thought those children were ugly and unlovable. In my immature mind, I even thought it was the fault of the parent and never wanted to be in their shoes. Now when I see a disabled child, it is painful because my son was in the same condition. My son wasn't scary and neither are they. I feel compassion and know that it could easily be my son in the wheelchair and wearing a neck brace.

We took Danny to several therapists, but all gave up on him, except for one. Marianne began working with Danny when he was six months old. She was very sweet and kind, and worked with Danny as much as she could. She had this way of making him move with massage, and he showed improvement. Occasionally, he would roll over, and it showed on his face that he was happy about it. He even started to react to the sounds of barking dogs and chirping birds.

Therapy was torture for him though. He would grunt loudly and his legs would shake after these exercises and sometimes I just couldn't stand there and watch. One day as Marianne exercised Danny; he reached out and patted the air, looking for something. He quickly found her hand and gave it a pinch.

"We don't pinch," she said, and moved his hand away. Her nickname for him was "Dan Dan." He loved her; he came alive with her, and was even able to crawl without help when she rubbed the back of his neck. We took him to see her every week unless he was sick in the hospital.

He was always in the hospital for weeks at a time. It was almost as though he had AIDS. Any eye infection or even a cold would put him in the hospital for two weeks. His immune system was very weak. His body temperature wasn't regulated, so sometimes his temperature would be 94 degrees, sometimes as high as 106 degrees. He suffered from constant seizures and needed medication every 8 hours. On the outside, Danny looked like a normal child for most of his first year. People would stop to ask how old he was, and I would shy away from them, because he was nine-months-old and still unable to sit up. I hated having to explain his sickness to curious strangers. People would try to give us advice on how to take care of him and I would get extremely defensive. Sometimes after a hospitalization I would go home, worn out mentally and physically and I would just bury my head into a pillow and scream until I felt better. I was strong for my son when I was around him, but inside I was scared and angry.

I quickly realized that Balázs was suffering as much as me. Although he didn't show his grief openly at the time, I can see the pain in his eyes in pictures we had taken back then. At first it upset me that he didn't show how much Danny's illness upset him. He stayed strong for all three of us, and remains the strongest person I have ever known. My husband helped keep me sane; he reminded me that Danny wasn't dead and that we had so much to be grateful for. We needed a positive attitude; and our love was enough motivation during these times. Some people claim that religion helped them through tough times, but it was our love that kept us together and motivated us to fight for our son.

I would break down every time I saw a healthy child with its mother. I was seeing everything I was missing out on and it made me feel like life was taunting me. This just made me angrier at God because I didn't have a normal parenting experience. I had given up on my faith the first time we were told that our son would never recover; and my husband, who was a new Christian at the time, had given up sooner than me. To this day, I have trouble with my belief in God, but am working on it. It is hard to trust God again after feeling so let down by Him.

Danny became critically ill when he was a year and a half old in the winter of 2002. He had developed pneumonia and blood poisoning beginning from a simple cold. He wouldn't eat and couldn't lift himself up. He had to get a CAT scan one day, and the screen showed that the chambers of his brain had expanded. I heard the doctor say, "What the hell is this?" when they saw the view of his brain. Later that night, I met with another doctor who sat across from me, and spoke in broken English.

"What do you think of your son's condition?" she carefully asked.

I wondered why she wanted to know. She looked at me with softness in her eyes and a pained expression, which was very strange, because this doctor had a very tough appearance. I never saw her look this way before.

"Do you know that he is close to death?" She asked in a surprised sounding voice. She was amazed that no one explained the results of my son's CAT scan. This was not the first time we had heard that our son was going to die. I felt sick. I craned my neck to see Danny in the next room. He pushed himself up and searched for me. This was the most activity I had seen him do in months.

"I don't understand. Look at him, he is pushing himself up," I said. "How can you know this anyway?" I asked. I hid the tears in my eyes, but they came out in my voice. She looked at me with wet eyes, and told me what the CAT scan revealed.

All I heard was, "He is going to die. Might be today, might be tomorrow. I know this is hard for you *anyuka*, because he was healthy at the beginning." I got up, walked into the hallway and crumbled as I waited for my husband to come and get me. We cried together in a darkened part of the hallway that night, as we talked to another English-speaking doctor and then we kissed our son and went home for the night.

Two months later, Danny died. After two years of constantly fighting for his life, he was gone. He died two weeks after his second birthday, and two weeks before we would have all come home to the States to get him to an American doctor. My husband and I stood by Danny's side in the hospital that last day with our hearts on the floor, as we watched our son pass away. Neither of us spoke. The same nurses who were there the day he came in sick as a three-week-old were there on that day. All the times he had been in the hospital I had the feeling he would survive, but this time I knew he would not. I put my head on my son's stomach and kissed him as his heart beat for the last time. He was freed from all his suffering and we lost our son to his second death.

The days after his death were unbearable. The first time I opened the cabinet to take out his clothes I cried. I held his clothing to my chest as though I was trying to stuff the hole that had been left. The day of his funeral we stood in the bitter cold and watched the small, white coffin with the words "Dan Dan" written on it, lower into the ground. My husband and I tightly held hands and stood there while his family came to kiss us. We stayed for an hour after everyone left, crying and touching the earth that covered him. The sun was shining, but I felt the sun had gone down on my life. I felt I would never laugh again, never live again. Words can't express how it feels to be a mother and then suddenly not be. You become a mother with no child.

❧

A week after our son's funeral, we moved to Colorado Springs, Colorado. We needed to live in a beautiful place to distract us from the ugliness that we had been through. We worked the same shift at a new job and spent our free time hiking in the mountains. Balázs didn't talk about Danny often, but I knew he was hurting. So, it helped me to talk about Danny to my family.

It was hard to know what to say when someone asked if we had children. I felt untrue to Danny by telling a stranger I had no children, but if I said I had one, I was lying too.

There is no way you can properly console someone who has lost a child. A lot of times people would say things to comfort us like, "My mother died, it has been hard for me too," "I had a miscarriage once" even "You are so young, you should have another baby." I am not saying that losing a mother or having a miscarriage isn't painful, but you can never compare grief. Everyone grieves in a different way, and even if someone had lost their child the same way as we did, they still wouldn't feel what we felt. Sometimes the only thing that helps is to have someone ask me what he was like, so I can talk about Danny's personality and I can have good memories to share. Sometimes it just feels good to have someone ask about him because it seems like they are interested in his life and not just his death.

A year after returning to the States, Balázs and I joined the Army. We found out we were expecting another baby six months after we got to our first unit. We were excited and scared at the same time. During our pregnancy, I worried and dreamt that our baby girl would get sick. I sanitized anything and everything in my house; I didn't eat certain meats and stayed away from most cheeses. I even called my doctor when I was on vacation because I was worried that I would expose the baby to germs by swimming in the ocean.

Our daughter, Gabriella, was born healthy and fat at 9 pounds. We didn't really start to relax and enjoy Gabby until she made it past her five week mark, completely healthy. She is a joy, and a handful. I am sure her big brother would have loved her and would have spent time teaching her new things.

Gabby has helped heal us in so many ways, and she brings an incredible amount of normalcy to our lives. It is a great thing that we had a second chance at becoming parents again.

౷

Before I had my son, I didn't have high aspirations, but after he died, I realized how fragile life is and if I have the ability to live and learn, I needed to make the most of my opportunities. Danny's passing inspired me to go to college and use my education to help people. Educating and comforting people who might be going through the same thing is actually helping me to heal. I want to give something to people that I feel might have helped me in my biggest time of need.

I know the strength we had to get through Danny's illness and losing him twice came from somewhere very deep inside us, and I can't explain how. Some might have even come from God.

Life does go on, but it takes a lot of strength, willpower and love to keep going. For now, I'm just taking things day by day.

Abigale Peszeki is a stay-at-home mother of 6-month-old Gabriella. She resides in Clarksville, Tennessee. Contact her at apeszeki@gmail. com

1 Abigale Peszeki
2 Excess fluid

Forgiving but Not Forgetting

By Kay Estes

"One word frees us from all the weight and pain
of life: that word is love."[1]

I was already crying.

It was time for my appointment, but the day I showed up at the clinic there were protestors outside enraged about the very thing I was there to do. After I checked in and the nurse called my name, I went to a waiting room in the back. This room was full of girls and each one had a story, some even similar to mine. While I waited I pondered the many factors that led to my decision and why I was there that day.

❧

About a year and a half after I graduated from high school and became a single mom, my boyfriend Dustin (now my husband), was deployed to Iraq when I had a life changing experience. I never thought I would have to go through the problems that followed.

It all started while I was staying at Jessica's one weekend. My infant daughter spent most of her weekends with her grandma allowing me some long awaited freedom. Jessica and I decided to go and see Jason, a trusted friend of ours. This particular night, the three of us figured we'd drink a bit and then go home.

I remembered having my first few drinks pretty fast. I wanted to feel carefree. I didn't have to worry about anything because Jason would never take advantage of me and Jessica always looked out for me. I began to feel the alcohol and then I noticed there were a lot of people showing up. But I didn't know any of those guys. And yes, most of them were men. What the hell was going on?

Jessica kept giving me drinks and told me that I would be fine. In a drunken state of mind, I simply believed her. I noticed after a particular drink that I was extremely tired. This wasn't just a typical drunken blackout. I couldn't keep my eyes open and the knot twisting around in my stomach was not going away. This was something more than the alcohol. I had been drunk enough before, and knew something was wrong.

Jess carried me outside but we had to stop so that I could puke. The smell was so nauseating. After Jess carried me back to a room to lie down, my next memory was of waking up next to a stranger.

The feeling of waking up half dressed next to someone I never met is so appalling. I started fighting this guy because I didn't remember the events that took place the night before. Had I been able to make logical decisions that night, I would never have had sex with anyone. He brought Jess in the room to tell me everything was okay.

Months later, Jess tried to explain how she left me with this strange guy to care for me while she went and got her groove on. I would have never left my best friend from middle school in the arms of a stranger so that I could party. I didn't understand her. I couldn't remember if I fought this guy off me or not during the rape. I was blacked out and believe someone slipped something in my drink.

About four to five weeks later I realized I might be pregnant. I felt very sick and remembered being that way while pregnant with my daughter. I didn't even have a memory of having sex with this guy. I felt so used and abused. I was raped and my rapist was a hardcore drug addict. How could he possibly care for a child? I felt betrayed by two of my friends who left me for nothing, but they weren't totally to blame. For starters, I never should have been there that night. I should have been at home trying to be a better mommy for my little girl.

What made things harder was that I had to hide the rape and pregnancy from my family. The night I found out I was pregnant; I was at Jessica's house. I was in denial about our "friendship" and her role in what happened. So, I still treated her as my best friend and talked to her about my pregnancy. She told me she would help take care of the baby if my mom kicked me out. One night that week, Jess called my mom and told her that I was pregnant and thinking of having an abortion.

My mom made me drive 30 minutes into town and buy a pregnancy test to take in front of her. She told me if she found out I was lying about not being pregnant, she would kick me out of the house. She threatened to take the car that her and my dad bought for me, which meant I would have no way to work or school. Also, I would have lost my daughter because I wouldn't want her to be homeless. To avoid all of that, I dipped the stick in the toilet water so that it would read negative.

I was so afraid my family would follow through with their threats and abortion was totally against their beliefs. I was 19-years-old, immature and very fearful. I knew if I talked to my mom about this, she would not have supported me. The idea of being a single mom on a low income with a deployed boyfriend and an undesirable birthfather all factored into my horrible decision to have an abortion. Although I was raped, I still felt attached to the baby. From day one, that little tiny speck on the ultrasound machine was a baby. He or she had a heart and was a real person. Could I really go through with this?

While I contemplated these factors, the nurse called six of us to go down to the basement.

The staff at the clinic made us go through about two hours of intense counseling. They explained in detail what was about to happen and then asked if this was our final decision. Though I was upset and still crying profusely, I had to go through with this. I went back to the waiting room until the nurse called my name to go into the procedure room.

Girls in the waiting room were discussing why they were there, some because it was a form of birth control, one because her mom made her do it as she was so young, another girl was raped, and some just weren't ready to be moms. As I sat next to a young lady describing her story, I found it was very similar to my own. I felt relieved that someone could relate to me.

Then the dreaded moment came and it was my turn. I was led down a long hallway and into a room where they sat me on a cold, metal exam table. I received an IV with medication to put me in a twilight sleep. The next thing I remembered was waking up.

In the recovery room, I sat beside my angel. This was the same girl I was next to in the waiting room. She was just another patient like me. I found it odd that out of all the patients in the clinic; I ended up next to this girl again. I felt as though she was sent to let me know that God forgave me for what I did. I just sat and cried while she held my hand. This young patient told me that when bad things happen to people, the hardest thing to do is forgive yourself. She held my hand until it was my turn to leave. Had I known her name, I would've thanked her for being my angel and watching out for me that day.

∾

After all this happened in October, I became pregnant by Dustin in February, but had a miscarriage. I do feel as though that was God's way of punishing me for the abortion. I became pregnant a fourth time in May and now have a little boy.

Learning how to get over an abortion is very hard. I still think about my baby and the hurt never went away. I will always remember my baby and wonder what could have happened. Sometimes I just sit and wonder "what if." If I had support at home from my parents and Dustin, then I would have at least given the baby up for adoption. But then I feel there is no way I wanted to lose Dustin and my daughter by having another baby. After all, my daughter's father left me when I became pregnant with her. I couldn't bear to have that happen again. Looking back, I realize I was being selfish.

I wanted to be happy and live my life and not have to deal with being raped or with being a single mom again. I just didn't think I could do it, but I wasn't willing to try either. My child would have been 2-years-old this year and I still have love for that baby and hatred toward myself for not having him or her. Although I still haven't forgiven myself, the important thing is I know God forgives me. I also know now that I am not the only person who has been raped and made this type of decision.

Although I believe abortions are unjustifiable and it was against my religion, I still made the decision. People say everything happens for a reason. Well, I felt like so much of what happened to me was my fault. I should have made more conscientious decisions about my extracurricular activities. I never thought about the bad things that could happen as a result. My focus was on the freedom that I finally had instead of on being a mother. If I had made wiser decisions, then I would not have even had to worry about an abortion. Being pregnant would not have been an option.

Deciding to have an abortion might seem like the right choice at the time, but the regret lasts a lifetime. During the first hours, it just takes a lot of energy to get off the couch and realize what your body just went through. As the days pass, it will become more of a reality. Some people will be very judgmental toward you, but it isn't their place. God is the one who we all will answer to one day.

There were times throughout the months and weeks that I just wanted to die. I hated myself for the horrible thing I did. I felt as though I didn't deserve to live. Seeing my beautiful children every day helps me to pull through it, although they cannot take the place of that baby.

Being the selfish person I am, I told Dustin about this situation after we were married. He stood by my side and has proven he will never leave me and I am now living life to the best of my ability. I'm in the process of finishing school and getting through each day, but this burden is still on my shoulders.

If you are still struggling with your abortion decision, I hope that you can get through this phase of your life. I've heard that there are post-abortion clinics, sometimes called crisis pregnancy centers, where you can get free confidential counseling. One day I hope to have the strength to get counseling, too.

If you had an abortion, I understand your hurt. I killed my own baby because I was selfish, afraid and hurting. Admitting that I did it is such a horrifying thought. I can only learn from what happened and try to help someone else through his or her time of need.

I hope that you can find some answers in the decision you made for not having your baby. It might seem as though none of the pain will ever go away. Talking to others who have been through similar situations helped me to deal with what happened.

There are people who support your decision but, despite that, the hardest thing is to forgive yourself. Being afraid, scared, and hopeless are all normal parts of an abortion. You just have to keep your head held high and know that you thought you were doing what was best for you and your baby at the time. Regret doesn't ever go away but take each day a step at a time and life and your happiness will get better. God loves you and so do I!

Kay Estes is a stay-at-home mom from Crofton, Kentucky. She married at the age of 20 and had two children by 21. She is fluent in sign language and hopes to finish college and work as an interpreter.

1 Sophocles

POPULATING HEAVEN
ONE ANGEL AT A TIME

By Carlo L. and Jacqueline Pike

"Though He slay me, yet I will hope in him." [1]

Jackie's story

We were a young African-American power couple and the first generation from both our families to complete a college education. Both of us came from broken homes and our main goal was to rewrite our family tree. We planned to groom our children with strong Christian values, a noble work ethic and lots of love. However, the Lord had a different plan for our lives. Our dreams of parenthood would be postponed when we lost nine babies within the first seven years of our marriage.

Carlo and I were married in July 1996 and soon after we moved to Chicago where my husband began medical school and I continued my undergraduate education at Aurora University. Although we were both students and money was very tight, I was filled with nothing but pleasant thoughts regarding our future. I couldn't wait for the day I could say I was a wife and mother.

About a year into our marriage we got pregnant for the first time. I can't say I was excited. Our first-year marriage issues had me doubting if we were ready for this huge responsibility. I married Carlo for his strong spiritual beliefs and unwavering faith in God. However, along with those beliefs came strong traditional values, as well. God is not only in the soul saving business; He also has a strong sense of humor.

He gave my husband a wife who didn't wash, clean, fold or cook. Who knew that after my long day of lectures, examines, study groups and a commute through Chicago traffic, Carlo would want a hot meal waiting on the table?

Although the news of this pregnancy wasn't met with overwhelming joy, we agreed this was going to be one beautiful and smart child. I had his or her life planned by the second week of my pregnancy. About a month into all of this joy, I went to the bathroom and saw blood. Instantly, my excitement turned to sadness. I knew what was happening. Within the next 24-hours we had lost our first baby. I felt horrible. I lay in the bed sobbing for hours. My husband did what he could to comfort me.

"God is in control of everything," he said. "This just wasn't our time." I thought *maybe he's right. We weren't ready to be parents yet. God knew that, so He took our baby to be with Him.*

But that first pregnancy lit a fire in me. Now, every time we made love, I wondered will this be the time that we'll conceive? I constantly had baby dreams. I was ready to prove to God that I could be a good mom.

Within six months, we were pregnant again. Things were great. I was taking my vitamins. I had gone to several doctor visits. Then at another routine visit when the doctor listened for the heartbeat, he couldn't find it. He seemed to get a little nervous and said he wanted to give me an ultrasound to make sure everything was alright. Believe it or not I got excited. I couldn't wait to see what my baby looked like. But there was no fetal movement or heartbeat found.

"Don't get upset," the doctor said. "Our equipment here is not that great. I'm going to send you to the local hospital so they can give you another ultrasound." Carlo and I drove to the hospital in complete silence. All I thought about was what will I tell everybody? I had told all my friends and family that I was pregnant. Now I have to tell them I lost my baby again. Tears began to fall from my eyes. Carlo laid his hand on my lap and said, "It's going to be okay."

At the hospital, they made me drink eight glasses of water. I felt like my bladder was going to burst. The doctor gave me another ultrasound and it was confirmed. There was no fetal heartbeat and no fetal movement. Our baby was dead. I never even knew if our baby was a girl or a boy.

After the ultrasound I emptied my bladder and saw blood. I fell to the floor and began to cry like I've never cried before. How could this be happening to me again? Why me? What did I do? I composed myself enough to walk out of the bathroom. Carlo and the doctor were waiting for me. I remember the doctor saying that we should schedule a D&C for the next day. He instructed me to go home and rest. How in the world could I rest with a dead baby floating around inside of me? That was truly one of those life changing moments.

After the surgery I was an emotional basket case. I would have hysterical breakdowns because the pain would get so bad. It often happened in church. I looked in front of me and I would see a baby. If I looked to my left, a baby. When I looked to my right, another baby. I would try to find a corner seat in the front of the church, but just when I thought I was safe, the next family to sit beside me would have a baby. My eyes would fill with tears. It felt as if someone had their hands around my throat. My heart would start to beat faster and faster. Eventually I would leave the sanctuary to prevent breaking down in front of everyone. On the way out the door I would see babies, babies and more babies.

I began to ask myself the same question over and over again, Father, why me? Why my babies? I promise if you give me a child, I will raise it up in your name and teach him or her about your endless love. Still, I often feel so helpless. I say the same prayer as often as I can, "Father, please bless our unborn babies." Soon my tears dry up and I'm able to go on with my day. Well, at least until the next time I'm in the grocery store, mall or family gathering and I see someone with their baby.

I've reached a point now where I can't cry. I'm actually out of tears, if that's possible. Can you imagine how it feels to be told time and time again, "Sorry, there's no heartbeat. Go home and rest, we'll call you as soon as we can to fit you in our schedule for a D&C."

For some reason all my babies would die within the first 10 to 12 weeks and each time it required surgery to remove the fetus. Each time they told us our baby wasn't alive, it felt like a bad dream. In the back of my mind I even began to expect to hear it. It's a horrible feeling to know you have a dead baby floating around in your belly with all the same symptoms as if you were still pregnant.

I felt like no one truly understood what I was going through. No one really knows what to say, so they say something stupid like "I told you to take it easy, some women just have to be on bed rest their whole pregnancy." As if I did this to myself. As if it's somehow my fault that all my babies keep dying.

My husband and my faith in God are what have kept me sane. That man loves me and I know it. Time and time again, after each loss Carlo has told me, "You're irreplaceable to me. I just want you." Even though I know his love is strong, I still have my insecure days. Sometimes I think maybe he would have been better off marrying someone who could give him a family. Someone who could give him a son that looks just like him with his big pretty eyes, large ears and wavy hair.

But, each time I'm feeling sorry for myself, I remember God loves me and doesn't want his children to suffer. I've been asked many times why Carlo and I tried so many times. Why didn't we just give up? My response to that question is, "faith." We have hope that God will allow us to be parents although the medical facts says differently.

At some point, I had to accept the possibility that I may never be a birth mother. I may never know what it feels like to have a healthy baby growing inside me. Or the feeling of a tiny foot kick me. But, I'm not going to let that stop me. I don't want to become angry and bitter. This painful experience is not going to crush my spirit or steal my joy.

All I can say is that time does begin to heal all wounds. The pain will become less and less sharp everyday. There are going to be days when it's hard to get out of bed. You may be drowning in self-pity and losing self-worth but, remember tomorrow is a new day. God will never give you more that you can handle. I am a much stronger person than ever before our losses. I may not have a child that looks exactly like me, but my life is filled with so many other blessing. Too many to count.

Carlo's story

We had always planned to adopt a child. We also discussed fostering children before we were married. I wanted to be a dad as long as I could remember. Still, we both understood that medical school, our finances and our busy schedules would not be a good setting to raise a child. I still do not know how or why we allowed ourselves to become pregnant that first time. I know we had discussed all the reasons why we should wait. We both agreed we were going to wait. Then it happened. Jackie was pregnant.

I was scared. I was struggling with school for the first time in my life. Everything that could go wrong was on its second time around and we were still newlyweds. We were poor and living in Chicago. The Army was paying for my tuition, books and fees but the stipend barely covered our rent. I was extremely frustrated and feeling a load of stress. I had failed one class and barely passed two others.

I wanted to be a Dad, but now was not the time. Jackie was already in shock from the reality of being a wife. I felt as if Jackie acted like a guest in our apartment. The shopping, cooking and cleaning were the responsibility of someone else - me. Suddenly some outside force was controlling her thoughts and decisions. Everything that we had agreed upon before marriage had become a topic of debate. We had several family members with views very different from our own. Jackie and I had agreed we wanted something different for our lives, but she was slowly being badgered, cajoled and criticized into living that same under-achieving lifestyle. I desired to be a father, but feared failing as a father more, and neither of us were ready for parenthood.

One of the first things taught in our OB rotations is that miscarriages are very common. So the first miscarriage, which occurred during my second year of medical school, was no big deal, for me. Honestly, it was a relief for one of the many mounting stressors. I reasoned that God was giving us a second chance to stick with our original plan of waiting until we were ready to start a family.

The second miscarriage hit Jackie much harder than the first. I had started to feel a little excitement about this pregnancy, but knew nothing else had changed in the short six-month span. I was again on the brink of failing a class; we had more bills and more debt but no more money. I told myself that God was using these losses to strengthen our relationship and grow our faith.

The hardest part of the second miscarriage was facing Jackie's deepening depression. I truly felt helpless. Nothing I said made her feel better. Any joyous moment shared by other parents or soon-to-be parents always led to more despairing moments for Jackie. As she fell deeper into despair, I felt more helpless and frustrated. I was failing at school, I was failing at becoming a father and I was wholly inadequate as a supportive husband. Although I could see the pain in her entire being, I could not escape the feeling of resentment and bitterness.

I was bitter towards Jackie because she had not been my idea of a "good wife," by preparing our home for a family. Why would God punish us for that and not the many others that were far guiltier? I harbored resentment toward all the worthless egg and sperm donors, mistakenly called parents, who were not caring for the children given to them by God. Now added to school, church, cleaning house and paying the bills, was the task of comforting a wife whose daily routine consisted of lying in bed, crying, and making expensive long distance phone calls that we could not afford.

I needed, or at least wanted, sexual healing all the time but Jackie needed affection and non-sexual intimacy, but I was 25-years-old and my other brain could not make the connection between sex, pregnancy, miscarriage, another surgery, more sympathy followed by questions and an even deeper depression for Jackie. Sure, I was studying medicine but my manhood was in question and I needed Jackie to confirm that it was still strong. I understood, intellectually, that Jackie needed to have her womanhood affirmed apart from her sexuality, but because I was so stressed and in need, I could not meet her needs.

It was not long before we were pregnant again. I was happy about the third pregnancy. It helped to lift Jackie out of her depression. She was as much afraid as she was excited. Everyone knew about the second loss and that compounded the pain. I asked Jackie not to tell anyone because I hated having to hear people comforting us, and we were both afraid of the possibility that miscarriage could happen again. There was no way I wanted to hear anyone trying to console us over another dead baby.

I hated hearing Jackie say she was keeping me from my dream of becoming a father. I would not accept the thought of never being able to father a child. I was not so worried about our plight not being fair; I just could not understand how any of it made sense. Surely, God knew that we would provide for and love a child more than any crack addict.

Once again, we found ourselves in the OB office. We were both nervous, but hopeful. This was the visit when we could expect to hear our baby's heartbeat. There was no way it could happen a third time, I reasoned. I was afraid to consider what a third miscarriage would mean. I was afraid to listen for the heartbeat but I was more afraid not to listen. We both needed this child to restore our hopes of parenthood.

It was not long before I realized there was again no heartbeat. I was confused, but don't think I was very emotional in the office. My mind immediately focused on the thought of sitting in the waiting room crying and praying that Jackie would wake up from the anesthesia after another D&C.

We left the hospital and it seemed as if it took forever to walk to the parking garage. I sat in the driver's seat and before I knew it, I was balling like a baby and could not stop. My small and unrealistic fear of never fathering a child was no longer small or unrealistic. We received the medical label, "habitual aborters." We would have to go through lab tests, questionnaires and physical exams. Now that I was training in the hospital and clinics, many of the people I interacted with daily would know about our recurrent losses. It was as if God wanted us to suffer pain and humiliation.

A part of me wanted to read and research everything I could find on the topic of Recurrent Pregnancy Loss, but the other part of me wanted to pretend the title was an inappropriate label for us. Therefore, that was what I did. I told myself that our three losses were simply random chance.

In John 9, Jesus' disciples asked, "Teacher, why was this man born blind? Was it because he or his parents sinned?" I asked similar questions of God more and more throughout our struggles. What have I done that you continue to take our children? Do you think this will make us stronger? Can you not see our hope is dying and our marriage is more troubled with each loss? God, why did you allow the crackhead's baby to live and our baby to die? Would you please tell me why?

Instead of answers, God kept adding painful questions. We have been through many more losses over the years. Oddly, Jackie and I do not agree on our total number of lost angels. My memory of the losses grew weak after we lost our third and forth child. I am convinced I have repressed most of those memories as a personal coping mechanism. I would need some type of mental and emotional shelter as we headed off to Fort Benning, Georgia for my intern year in a family practice residency. Jackie had started doing most of the cooking and cleaning by that time. She even ran an in-home child care business to help pull us out of debt. I was working at the hospital so much, I am sure she felt neglected and abandoned.

We had four or more losses while I was in residency training. By the time I completed my residency training, Jackie and I were both clinically depressed and frustrated. We had been to reproductive specialists in three states. Jackie has had surgeries to correct possible causes but in the end, none of the specialist has had an answer for us. Often times, their response is that everything is normal. Of all the possible descriptions of our struggles with miscarriages, normal could never be appropriate. More and more questions continued to gnaw on my heart. I have had to evaluate and counsel countless infertile couples throughout my training and now in my practice. Is it a test? Maybe God is laughing at us. I am certain that Satan is. Perhaps it is all simply meaningless. That is what Solomon says in the book of Ecclesiastes. "Meaningless! Meaningless!"

says the teacher. "Utterly meaningless! Everything is meaningless."

Somehow, I still believe that one day we will give birth to a healthy baby. I am not sure why I believe. I question myself but never have an answer. Job said, "Though He slay me, yet will I trust Him." God has been our one constant and He has always made a prosperous end out of our most despairing trials. I keep asking and expecting Him to do the same in this situation.

Four months after I became board certified in family practice, I received a call from one of my colleagues that would forever change our lives. Some might consider it a coincidence that this was just after our income jumped close to six figures and we had moved into the home we had built in Tennessee. So there we were in a big house with big money and Jackie kept asking if I was still considering adoption. It just so happened that this colleague from Georgia had a young patient who, along with her mother, were looking for a couple to adopt the girl's baby. Her expected due date was more than a month away. Two weeks later, our precious little princess was in Jackie's arms. She is the most wonderful baby girl in the world and I would not trade her for ten thousand babies or a life without the memories of miscarriages. She is now almost three-years-old and I cannot imagine a child blessing a family as she has blessed ours.

Some say that God does not always answer prayers. Well, I say He is so good at making masterpieces out of our limited requests that we often do not recognize them when He has finished His response!

Carlo L. Pike is a soldier and family practice physician working at Fort Campbell, Kentucky. His wife, Jacqueline, is a stay-at-home mother to their 2-year-old daughter. She stays active in the Officer's Spouse Club, Protestant Women of the Chapel and community activities.

1 Job 13:15

I'm Still a Mother

By Sharee Moore

*"For I have learned, in whatsoever state I am, therewith
to be content."*[1]

My husband and I were moving to Hawaii, but, I barely learned to say "aloha" before I found myself coiled in a grief so intense, I thought I'd surely have a stroke.

Within months of settling into our new home, everything that was me thudded into my lap, wrapped in a tiny lifeless bundle. We weren't ready to face what lie ahead because, as a family, we still grappled with the sudden death of Cory, my 20-year-old brother. Cory's passing crippled us, but when my two cousins, James and David, died less than a year later, the combined hurt crushed our spirits.

I guess some folks turn to God during times of trouble. I didn't. Later, I found it would take more than a nice personality to get through the worst days – months – and years – of my life.

My husband, Henry, and I were positively radiant with pregnancy. We were so happy that we would now be complete. We were new to Hawaii and didn't have a social network, let alone a spiritual one, so when I went into preterm labor in August of 2002, Henry and I clung to each other. I was only 23 weeks pregnant.

We rushed to labor and delivery, where we learned my cervix already dilated 3 centimeters. I spent five days lying head-down, while doctors pumped me full of labor-halting drugs. The magnesium sulfate burned a path through every vein and capillary in my body. Since I lay in an unnatural position, it seemed that food and my internal organs drifted toward my throat, making it difficult to breathe or swallow. My body swelled as it held on to extra water; and I grew even more hot, nervous and hopeless. I had little to no faith that everything would work out, but felt even worse for Henry. He had to watch me suffer while he battled his own fears. I wanted to send Henry away, but I desperately needed him there.

At that point, the emotional and physical burdens of trying to preserve our son's life were driving me insane. I knew Christopher only had a 10 percent chance of survival if he were born at 24 weeks. I felt frustrated and scared, but was too delirious from the drugs to cry and when I tried to talk about the pain, my speech slurred. I had the common sense to pray for a way of escape, but it came in an unexpected form. Relief came when Christopher was born.

He was 23 weeks, 5 days and weighed only 1 pound. Every hour, our son fought for his life in the neonatal intensive care unit. While spending every moment by his side, I fought for my sanity. I prayed and cried. Prayed and cried. Then I just gave up and cried.

On Christopher's eighth day, we knew he wouldn't survive because his little organs began to fail and the skin along his chest and back began to die. The only thing that kept the hospital from pulling the plug on the ventilator were the needs of two desperate, praying parents. The staff knew all hope was lost. Our prayer at this point went from "God, save Christopher," or "Please God, take me instead," to "Please just let Christopher look at us."

That day, Christopher opened his eyes for the first time. God answered us when we were desperate for *anything*. We were crying out, "Lord just give us something to cling onto!"

When Christopher's eyes opened we knew God had heard all our prayers, He just didn't answer "yes" to each one. I don't know why, but Henry and I both had peace with that.

Ten days after his birth, Christopher released two tiny rattled breaths and died in my arms. My once lofty optimism plummeted to my feet. I wanted to smash, burn and destroy something – or someone. I hollered at God in despair, "Why not take me? How can I live when my son is dead?" I was angry with God, but hated myself. My body failed at a time when Christopher needed me most. I gave in to a depression so deep and dark, light couldn't penetrate it. I howled until spit and tears soaked my shirt, my pillow and my days.

Although I couldn't forgive God at the time, He began to place people in my life that began to fertilize the rocky soil in my heart. He sent others who planted His Word in that soil and still, He sent another person who watered.

I'd love to report that I was just fine after that, but I still struggled with depression. I couldn't get out of bed. I had night sweats and nightmares. Psychotherapy and medications didn't work. I kept my scream inside but thought another baby would fill the void inside me. As I snuggled deeper into grief, Henry lost both his son and his wife. A baby became my new focus and obsession. I cared little for anything, or anyone else. Three months after Christopher died, I was pregnant again.

It was 2002 and I'd barely settled into the joy of pregnancy when, on Christmas Day, I had a miscarriage. We chose not to tell anyone about this pregnancy because we feared others' reactions. After the miscarriage, we vowed never to get pregnant again; the pain was too great. The depression resurfaced, but miraculously – so did my pregnancy. Lab results and an ultrasound revealed that our baby was still alive!

Oh, can I even describe our joy? Our new friends celebrated with us every step of the way. Understandably, our immediate family was a little less enthusiastic. My parents still mourned my brother and now they had a grandson to add to the list. Maybe they thought we were adding to their pain, but we needed this baby. I needed this baby.

Each passing week unearthed a new emergency, which created more fear. The miscarriage occurred because one twin died. Other irregularities were given medical terms I later looked up on the Internet. In March 2003, the doctors said I needed to have a cerclage[2] placed. After the surgery, I spent two and a half months on strict bed rest.

God laid me in that bed to groom me for His perfect will. He prepared my heart and mind for the future trials we would face. I learned more about Jesus and his expectations. Most of all, I thanked him for blessing us with a baby.

I was 24.5 weeks pregnant when I went into preterm labor again. It was May of 2003 and all I could think was, *Oh no! Not again! We can't handle another loss.* We questioned, "God who are you? How can you allow this to happen? What sin has required the loss of two sons, a brother, and two cousins - within two years?"

At 25 weeks gestation, an emergency c-section was necessary to save our son's life. He only weighed 2.5 pounds, but Kasimir was perfectly formed and bursting with energy. He had a full head of hair and the most beautiful face I'll ever know. I was worried about our son, but assumed that because he was bigger than Christopher, he would survive. By the end of day one, Kasimir was pretty much breathing on his own.

On the morning of day two, I awoke early excited about the prospect of pumping milk. While I arranged the bottles, a nurse rushed into my room to announce Kasimir was in distress and it didn't look like he would make it.

I was in denial. I remembered how often our first son went into distress and look how long he lived. I flat-out refused to worry. After all, I had checked on my baby less than six hours ago and he was fine. He flailed his tiny arms and wrinkled his face in a silent cry. The nurse wheeled me to the NICU and my husband joined us 15 minutes later. After a late night, he had gone home to shower and get some rest.

A team of nurses and doctors huddled around Kasimir, but I prayed. I ignored the trilling alarms and angrily flashing lights. I knew God didn't carry us through a real-life drama only to have our son join his heavenly flock. But I was wrong.

The doctor summoned us to a backroom reserved for disturbing announcements. As we slumped on the couch, the doctor's eyes welled with tears. He explained that Kasimir lost too much blood when a capillary burst in his lung. The only method of stopping this type of bleeding didn't work. He was sorry. The staff kept Kasimir alive just long enough for me to gather his limp body in my arms.

When Henry saw his son, he let loose a wail that could have made our 200 year-old ancestors cringe if they could hear. I just stood there like a mound of nothing – numb, dumb and cold.

Once I came home from the hospital I couldn't get out of bed. The scream began scratching at my insides again and I wondered how I would survive this loss. Henry seemed so strong; I never thought he wouldn't be okay, but I wouldn't make it. As I was about to free fall into the darkness, a dear friend shared a lesson I'll pass along to you.

Beverly said, "For the believer, this life is temporary. All the hurts and disappointments are only a test. Now, would I pass this test and grow in Christ or, would I fail and have all that I've been through been for nothing?" I then asked myself, can I live knowing that my babies died for no reason? I practically screamed "NO!"

I picked myself up out of that bed of affliction and made it my goal to know God simply for who He is. Daily, I repented, prayed, and studied my Bible, applying His truth to my life. I actually got excited about Jesus and got re-baptized in His name. God filled me with the Holy Spirit and my life changed! I knew I had God on the inside because when I prayed, I spoke in a heavenly language.

I wanted my life and situation to suddenly become perfect, but it didn't. My life changed in stages. It took about five months before I could laugh without feeling guilty. Every night I lay down knowing it was my body that snuffed out two babies' lives. Also, I believed my weak body kept my husband from becoming a dad. I'm still trying to heal from that.

Once I allowed it to happen, joy eventually replaced my sorrow and depression; and self-forgiveness overshadowed guilt and shame. Once I forgave myself, I decided to forgive others who had hurt me in the past. Whether it was my father who rejected me, friends who disappointed me or the respiratory technician who didn't intubate my son correctly – I forgave them all. Forgiving others was an important step and in those moments, I experienced a peace that is indescribable.

Over time, I asked God to fill me with love, which replaced the anger and hate I held for my situation and the jealousy I felt for so-called undeserving moms. I sometimes dreamed that a teen mom or somebody would want to give me their baby. I had to learn to change that obsession into something good.

For me, more than a spiritual transformation took place. Emotionally, I became more interested in caring for my husband, home and others. I began to see past my loss and notice others' pain. Physically, I became more active. God also healed my lungs, which were plagued with a respiratory disease. Many of these changes gradually took place between October 2003 and March 2004, but continue to this day.

You may say, "God loves us too much to ever take our children, our health or those things we hold dear." I say to you, God loves us so much he sent His son to DIE, and we, as believers *will suffer.* It is through our suffering we are made perfect, established, strong and settled.[3]   The secret to receiving the promised strength is to believe and stay focused on God *throughout the trial.*

This fact was revealed to me when we suffered a stillbirth in November 2005. In my utter and complete confusion, I only knew one thing; I would not forsake God. Although Henry was deployed to Iraq and I suffered through 33 hours of labor, in the company of strangers; God still showed me His love and mercy.

He showed me love through Jane, who spent the night, cared for me and coordinated my life from a hospital room. I didn't know her before that day.

I saw God's love through the nurses, B.J. and Kristin who showered me with hugs and treated me as though I were the only patient they had. God touched me through the hospital chaplain, David, who tended my spiritual needs and fed my desire for comfort food. And through my sister, Tianja, who didn't ask, "Is there anything you need?" Instead she said, "I'll be there, tomorrow."

I love the Lord and won't turn from Him, but that doesn't mean I'm pain-free. I still struggle with the ugly side of grief. It used to shackle me to the bed, but now it's the Holy Spirit who gives me the strength to get up every morning. I used to focus on myself and the magnitude of my pain, now I can reach out to other hurting women.

My due date would have been the week I write this to you. I admit, it is hard to stop wanting what I don't have, but I'm learning to be content with what I *do* have. I have vibrant health, a compassionate husband, and a loving family. Most importantly I have a relationship with Jesus.

This is where the real story begins.

Sharee is a mother of three heaven-bound babies, wife of one and receives inspiration from many. She is a counselor, self-publisher, writer, editor and servant of the Lord. She can be reached at momax3angels@yahoo.com

---

1 Philippians 4:11 (KJV)

2 A procedure designed to surgically close the cervix so it doesn't open before the baby reaches full-term.

3 (1 Peter 5 9-10) states [9]Whom resist stedfast in the faith, knowing that the same afflictions are accomplished in your brethren that are in the world. [10]But the God of all grace, who hath called us unto his eternal glory by Christ Jesus, after that ye have suffered a while, make you perfect, stablish, strengthen, settle you.

Part Four

FOR THE FUTURE

TRIED AND TRUE STRATEGIES FOR TODAY, TOMORROW, THE FIRST YEAR AND BEYOND

The first hour

The first day

The first weeks

The first several months

What's next: What to expect when you're grieving

Pain relief: What's worked for others

The truth about grief: The real deal

Unhealthy grief: How to tell if you may need extra help

Some friendly advice: If you're a friend ... here's how

you can help

The first year and beyond

Children and grief

THE FIRST HOUR:

Seek comfort. Find the nearest person and let them hold you - whether it is your spouse, a nurse, friend, the chaplain or even the doctor. One mom recommends spending that time in prayer and deep meditation. Another mom took the phone off the hook, and took time for herself. For once, don't put others' needs ahead of your own. Do what works for you during difficult times and put words to what you need from others.

THE FIRST DAY:

Spend time with your baby. Take as much time as you need to hold your baby after he or she has died. It will help transition from loving them as earthly bodies, to loving them as spirits. Take pictures, if that is an option. If your baby died in the intensive care or soon after delivery, gather every item used to care for your baby during her short life. Also, do what you can to parent your baby for the last time. You might talk to your baby, change her diaper, dress him or wrap him in a blanket. Don't try to work or drive a car or watch your other children by yourself. Find a friend or companion to be with you. Talk to a nurse about what to do about your milk coming in, and the discomfort of swollen breasts. Find any spark of a happy thought and cling to it. One minute at a time, one step at a time, know that you will make it through this day, and the next and the next. See the *Additional Reading* section for Web sites offering a more detailed list of options.

THE FIRST WEEKS:

Enlist help. Ask loved ones to send notes, mass e-mails, inform neighbors, and act as your support network. Also allow them to help make funeral or memorial service arrangements, answer phones, prepare food and clean the house.

Do something to publicly remember your baby. With early miscarriage, you usually cannot cradle or bury your child, but you can light a special candle, hold a memorial service, build a luminary, plant a garden, create a quilt from baby clothes, start a journal in their memory, or begin a new family tradition in your baby's honor.

Suggestions:

• For step-by-step instructions for creating a memorial garden, visit: www.uvm. edu/pss/ppp/articles/memorial.html

• For a variety of infant loss memorial items such as jewelry, sun catchers, garden decorations, figurines and more, visit: www.littleangelsonlinestore.com

• Read *Surviving Holidays, Birthdays & Anniversaries: A Guide for Grieving During Special Occasions* by Brook Noel for more ideas.

Handling your baby's stuff. An empty nursery is a painful reminder of what is gone. I'm not suggesting you throw those items away or not plan for the possibility of future children, but give yourself a set time to package and store all the baby items. Put a few treasured items in a safe place, until you are healed enough to put them on display. As long as the sight of those baby items triggers uncontrolled crying or depression, consider putting them away. Don't batter yourself if you feel unable to take this step at this time. There is no right or wrong timeframe.

Set a slower pace and simplify your tasks and your life. If you just suffered a loss, now isn't the time to go back to school or begin a complex project at work. Feeling overwhelmed, forgetful and tired are normal reactions when you are grieving. The combination may cause frustration once you realize you can't operate in your normal capacity.

Eat healthy. If you don't feel like preparing meals from scratch using the food groups, purchase fresh, conveniently packaged foods that contain them. There are bagged fresh vegetables and fruits, shredded and sliced cheeses and ready-to-bake lean meats. For easy-to-use tips about proper nutrition, visit the National Cancer Institute's Web site at www.5aday.gov/index.html. Department of Agriculture sports an interactive food pyramid on its Web site at www.mypyramid.gov/pyramid/. Also listed are specific formulas about how much to eat from each food group based on age, gender and physical activity.

Get plenty of exercise and rest. The Centers for Disease Control and Prevention Web site states that regular physical activity reduces depression and anxiety. A simple plan might include just 30 minutes of brisk walking five or more times each week. Visit the Department of Health & Human Services Web site at www. smallstep. gov for bite-sized tips and a customized fitness plan.

Join a support group. This is a very important step. Most people outside of a support group will feel uncomfortable facing your loss. Most will avoid you or grow impatient with your inability to "get over it." Members of a support group never grow tired of your inner turmoil and your daily struggles. If they are a good group, they will offer suggestions for how to work through pain and will help identify harmful grieving patterns. As you listen while others share, you'll learn that you aren't going down a path that's never been traveled. It will also do wonders for lowering your fear and anxiety. To find a support group near you, call the information desk at the local hospital, use the yellow pages, do an Internet search, ask your doctor or, if you qualify for military benefits, contact the closest services organization on the installation. The *Additional Reading* section contains a list of organizations.

THE FIRST SEVERAL MONTHS:

Release your emotions. Identify your feelings and then express them for a minimum of 15 – 20 minutes each day. Release may come through journaling, screaming, running, or beating a pillow. Give in to whatever feels right as long as it isn't physically, mentally or spiritually harmful to yourself or others. Be honest about how you feel and clear your mind in order to make healthy choices about your life.

Make this "release time" a scheduled part of every day.

Choose not to give up. Some grieving parents have asked, "What is the point of living if my baby is dead?" Maybe you feel that way, too. Try thinking of it in another way. What if it were you who died and your baby who survived? Really spark your imagination and make this scenario feel realistic. What if you could observe your child lying around despondent, uninterested in life or the wonderful opportunities and experiences to be had? Year after year, you watch your child grieving your death. You watch them crying over your belongings, setting up a shrine in your memory, camped out at the gravesite, turning from family and friends, depressed, medicated and in a constant state of pain. Now you have one moment to tell them something. What would you say? Write it down in great detail. If you are totally honest, this may lead to a breakthrough for you. Next step: Take your own advice.

Seek intimacy with your spouse. Try to view lovemaking as a way to draw closer, have fun and relieve stress, not just as a tool to "get another baby." Be gentle with each other, reduce expectations but acknowledge that lovemaking is important to your relationship. Do not allow weeks or months to pass without reaching out or responding to your partner's sexual advances. Even when you "don't feel like it," demonstrate physical love and compassion for your mate. Men: Initiate cuddling, hugging, non-sexual touching and uninterrupted "listening time." This will do wonders for increasing her sexual desires. If either of you suspect depression is cooling your flames, seek professional treatment from a counselor or medical professional. Read more about the signs and symptoms of depression in the section *SOME FRIENDLY ADVICE: If you are a friend ... here's how you can help,* or visit the National Institute of Mental Health Web site at www.nimh.nih.gov.

Allow family and friends to be a part of your life. Sometimes a friend may reach out, but you may not feel like company right now. It's okay to say no to visitors, but let them know you appreciate their concern and give them a day that you will accept visitors – then follow through. If you push family and friends away or pretend everything is okay, you may find yourself alone, indefinitely and in a pit of depression.

Tell people how you feel. Share how you really feel. Let them know how they can help you. Ask others to initiate a conversation about your baby, invite you out to a movie, walk or dinner. Develop a network of people who can be there for you when others just don't have the courage. A variety of online agencies are found in the *Additional Reading* section of this book.

Avoid isolation. Return to work as soon as you are physically and mentally able. If you were planning to stay home before tragedy struck – go to work as a volunteer or seek employment. Isolating yourself without a constructive outlet may lead to depression and added feelings of loss because you feel your life has lost purpose. Other unproductive and unhealthy behaviors may also develop like: sleeping the day away, watching television all day and eating, just to eat. Employment provides meaning and gives a break from grieving 24-hours a day. It gives us a mission, but shouldn't be used to "skip" the grieving process. There is no getting around grief.

After two months pick up the pace - a little. Some may say no one can dictate when a person should move forward, but real life experience (I lost three infants in three years) has taught me that to sit home without a purpose invites the 3 D's: **d**isaster, **d**epression and utter **d**ismay. If you haven't gone back to work, now may be a time to consider it. Again, be gentle with yourself. You probably won't feel like doing much of anything short of staring and sleeping, so enlist the help of a compassionate friend. If you don't have one, contact me (Sharee) at: www.stolenangels.com.

Ease guilt. To relieve guilt, get as much information about your pregnancy, your baby's condition or your medical history as possible. For miscarriage, seek more advanced medical advice or treatment. Sometimes we need to hear a doctor say we aren't to blame for our baby's demise, premature birth, illness or genetic condition. Rest assured there will come a time when guilt will lessen, and even go away, but you have to be able to discuss it, process it, and eventually be willing to release it. Experiencing guilt is all a part of the grief process. One young mother woke up next to her baby and he wasn't breathing. She did CPR, called for help and got a neighbor to dial 911. She couldn't shake the questions – did I roll on my baby during the night? Did I do CPR wrong? Did he get sick from something I fed him? Did my diet during pregnancy cause some sort of birth defect? It wasn't until she received the autopsy and police reports, interviewed doctors, the chaplain and the coroner that she was able to release much of her guilt. The information empowered her to move forward. No one can take your guilt away from you. It is a real feeling and best dealt with through prayer and by talking to a trusted therapist specializing in grief and loss.

Go where there is laughter. Okay, so you may not feel like laughing. Understandable, but there is something healing about laughter. Studies have shown that laughter causes a chemical release of natural pain killers, called endorphins. Laughing lowers blood pressure, reduces stress hormones, increases muscle flexion, boosts infection fighting cells, and more. Read more at www.holisticonline.com and click "humor therapy." Also visit www.psychologytoday.com and type "laughter" into the search tool.

Handling the due date blues. Most moms expressed feelings of anger, self-loathing and intense sadness during the days leading up to their due date. Some moms sat in silence and felt a quiet depression. One mom remembers crying and fantasizing about all the things she should have been doing on that date. Others didn't experience due date blues, but felt more of a connection to the date their baby died. To get through this period, realize that your feelings are normal. Try to honor your baby by creating new memories outside of your house. Plan a weekend getaway and talk about your child, allow family members to comfort you and know that others have worked through the intense grief you now experience, and so will you.

WHAT'S NEXT: What to expect when grieving

Painful reflections. You will probably relive the days, hours and moments leading up to your loss. This may happen through nightmares, "daymares" or triggered by a sight of a pregnant woman, lone child or even the smell of your favorite pregnancy food. A sad song, commercial or even a picture can also cause a painful reflection. It can happen anytime, anywhere.

"If only ..." moments. If only I had taken it easy, if only I hadn't smoked that cigarette. If only I hadn't had that abortion eight years ago, if only I hadn't waited to go to the hospital, If only I would have checked on my baby sooner, if only ...

Expect others to believe you're superwoman or superman. Friends and family may think you have this tremendous strength or faith simply because you "look good" on the outside. On the inside expect to feel stark raving mad, at times.

Expect others to <u>not</u> notice your pain. When the pain felt so profound I often wondered how others couldn't see it. They know I lost a baby three months ago, how can they imagine I'm not hurting today? There are several reasons why: First, we try very hard to put up a brave front. Sometimes, we don't realize how convincing we really have been. Second, people fear they may "remind" us of our loss if they bring it up. Third, a person may feel uncomfortable with your grief or wrestling with their own pain.

Expect to feel offended by others' seemingly trivial concerns. You'll want to compare most situations with your loss and of course, in your mind, their pain or frustrations will never measure up. We encourage you to cut people some slack.

Expect to want others to open up around you and talk about their babies, lives, struggles. On the flip side, you may find yourself offended or tired of hearing about their babies, lives and struggles! Again, cut them some slack and understand that your trauma has changed your views about a lot of things.

Expect to have outbursts. There may be times you want to scream at your neighborhood, "Look at me! Can't you see I'm hurting?" Usually they can't see it. A support group really comes in handy at times like these. You can call someone who does actually understand.

Expect others to expect you to guide them through your grief. Just hand them a copy of this book, or tell them (with love) what is on your heart.

Expect relationship troubles. Friendships with other pregnant women may grow strained. Your intimate moments with your spouse may become more about "getting pregnant again" than about closeness and love. Communication can crumble if you don't understand the differences between how people mourn. But all isn't lost – open communication and the passage of time are excellent ingredients for healing. See the *Additional Reading* section at the back of the book for a list of books and Web sites that may prove useful.

Expect that you'll have to make decisions about your baby's stuff. Should you box items up, give them away, take them back to the store, throw everything out or leave them be for a while? These are only a few of the questions you'll wrestle with. Putting these cherished items away doesn't mean you're trying to forget your baby or that they aren't important.

Expect that your family and friends' lives will move on. The world will continue as if nothing has happened. Try not to be mad at others who are no longer mourning.

PAIN RELIEF: What's worked for others

Call out to Jesus. Literally cry and ask God (aloud) to ease your pain.

Find a firm shoulder to cry on. Husbands, boyfriends, fathers and friends work well. Men: Don't underestimate the healing power of crying with your spouse.

Cry. Hard with wailing, thrashing, slobber and snot. It really works.

Go to sleep. You'll feel well rested and it is a simple escape. Rotate sleep with other activities.

Avoid or remove painful reminders from your sight. It may hurt to pack up all those precious baby items, but it may spare you added grief later. I don't recommend throwing items away, just consider putting them out of sight – for now. Don't do this alone. Ask someone to help or at least be there with you.

Accept that we can never undo what has been done. We cannot restore that which has been lost – not in a human form anyway. But we can choose to live a life that brings a joy and peace for ourselves and others. In your heart and mind make the decision to live – truly live - although your baby's life has ended. Take a peek at the *Additional Reading* section for books to help you through this stage.

Don't get stuck in depression. Know the signs of depression and don't be afraid to ask a friend to help keep an eye out for its symptoms, too. Symptoms are listed in the section titled *SOME FRIENDLY ADVICE: If you are a friend ... here's how you can help*, or on the National Institute of Mental Health Web site at www.nimh.nih.gov. Seek professional help, if you are concerned for yourself.

Add another dimension to your love. A kitten, puppy, plant or a close friend's baby could never replace your child, but some have found caring for someone or something else helps fill the void. We don't recommend getting pregnant right away. Physical healing is important, but could you handle the emotional devastation of another loss? One writer shared that she carries a Doppler everywhere so she can keep tabs on her unborn baby's heart beat. Another mom cannot bear to let her second child out of her sight because she is afraid something may happen to him. A third writer suffered a second loss, immediately after the first and hasn't been the same since. We mention these situations so that you know there are alternatives to having a baby right away ... try a puppy and see how you feel! Visit www. puppyanddog.com to take a quiz and see which breed would be best for you. Read more at: http://healing.about.com/od/askkim_qa/f/whatbreedog.htm (there is an underscore between 'askkim' and 'qa'). Then go search for your "love companion" at a local animal welfare or rescue agency. Visit: www.pets911.com to search for an agency near your home.

Learn to jog. If it has been six weeks since you delivered or had a miscarriage and if you've been cleared by your doctor – go for it. Running provides a psychological release from stress and a bad attitude. It also builds your confidence and character while providing something better than prescription medications – a runner's high. Sprinting will allow you to burn up anger and frustration. A long run will give you time to mull through some of those unanswerable questions raging through your mind. A light jog will help beat fatigue and it has been used to even treat clinical depression. Experts say that when you prove that you can overcome an obstacle on a run (like a big hill, long distance or improve your time) you also build the confidence to face other obstacles in your life. To receive a free, customized training program to get you started, visit www.runnersworld.com then click on "Training" and follow the directions from there. If jogging isn't your thing, add a new form of exercise instead.

Cultivate a new circle of friends. Bereaved parents have found comfort from others who understand their loss and to whom they can talk freely. Try a support group or one of the online communities listed in the *Additional Reading* section.

Don't compare your loss to others' or theirs to yours. Trying to determine "who hurts more" is insulting and doesn't do much to comfort you or them. We see this a lot when a miscarriage is compared with a SIDS case or umbilical cord accident. From the moment one discovers they are pregnant, no parent expects their child to die. And no parent expects an opportunity to prepare for this type of tragedy. The pain each parent experiences is very real and debilitating, but the way in which each parent mourns is different. The parent of a 2-year-old will mourn quite differently than the parent of a stillborn baby.

As parents, we all experience intense pain and confusion, but parents whose babies were older will reflect on concrete memories of their loved one – her smile, the sound of his cry, how she clung to your hip or neck, his personality traits and other intensely happy and sad moments. A parent who left the hospital with empty arms may reflect on the hopes and dreams for their child. The kicks, jabs and flutters also seem to take on a special meaning.

Grieve fully. We must grieve fully in order to move forward with life. If you don't, a part of self becomes caught in the past and the pain that isn't released will always stand in the way of really living. One mom just felt tired of crying, but she knew tears were an important way to release the pain. To help trigger those healing tears, she would listen to sad songs on the *City of Angels* soundtrack or watch a sad movie like *Terms of Endearment.*

Use prayer to heal. Some say praying to a "higher power" is the answer, but the parents (featured in this book) who've returned to wholeness specifically had a belief in and a relationship with Jesus Christ.

THE TRUTH ABOUT GRIEF: Here's the real deal

You are not crazy. You're just different from who you were before this loss. We feel abnormal or "crazy" because now there may be memory loss, inability to focus and we aren't conforming to others' timelines for when we should be done mourning. Sometimes we're happy, the next day we may feel depressed. One week we're making progress, the next we just want to sleep the pain away. A normally affectionate parent may feel emotionally unavailable toward surviving children, or you may feel more compassionate than your "old" self. Everything feels out of whack right now, but there will be a day when you will experience a new normal. For me, it took about three years before the stretches between painful moments grew so far apart, I could almost say I was pain free. Thomas Ellis, author of *This Thing Called Grief: New Understandings of Loss*, describes it this way: Whatever our experience is today, we begin to learn that it will most likely be different tomorrow. This is not about clear, predictable "stages." Rather, it is a natural process of dynamic changes with the power to ebb and flow as it may. Grief will not follow a neat or logical order.

Anger is normal. Feel it, accept it, but choose to release it. Anger may cause you to blame God, the doctor, your mother and your friends. Just know your negative feelings are normal, so try not to deny that you feel them. If you struggle with anger, pick up a copy of Brook Noel's book *Grief Steps: 10 Steps to Regroup, Rebuild and Renew After Any Life Loss*

Feelings of insecurity are normal. Your self-esteem has taken a bashing and you may feel like you failed as a mother and a wife. As a father you may feel hopeless because you couldn't protect your wife or baby.

To stop grieving doesn't mean you've forgotten. If you do the grief work and heal, you can begin to remember with love, not pain.

Healing is hard work. It's easier to do absolutely nothing, live in the past, sulk and feel sorry for yourself. The hard work is coming to terms with your loss. It is hard to pack up the nursery. It is hard to face the waiting room full of pregnant moms when it is time for your follow up exam. It is hard to join family and friends in celebration of birthdays, baby showers, holidays and other special occasions. It is hard to just plain get out of the bed – and stay out. For all your hard work, reward yourself. Splurge on something frivolous. Get highlights in your hair, a pedicure, a hot stone massage, visit the spa, or begin a new hobby – whether it is Pilates, gardening or stained glass art! It isn't a magic cure, it won't replace your angel, but it can be one healing moment on a hard path to wholeness.

How you pass the time lessens the pain. It takes an enormous amount of time and work to heal our hurt and our hearts. One cannot lie down in despair and hope for the pain to simply vanish. Pray for relief and take the meaningful steps suggested in this chapter to clear your mind and unburden your soul. Despite your feelings today, the pain really will lessen through faith and your effort.

UNHEALTHY GRIEF: How to tell if you may need extra help

No progress – at all. If after several weeks or longer you aren't moving through the grief at all and there is no relief from the pain. In the book, *Facing the Ultimate Loss: Coping with the Death of a Child* by Robert J. Marx and Susan Wengerhoff Davidson, the authors provide a list of warning symptoms:

• If you can't speak about your angel without experiencing the same level of intense sadness you felt when you found out about his or her passing.

• If you are determined to leave the nursery exactly as it is and you experience rage, frantic behavior or panic if anything is touched or moved.

• If you exclude people from your life who knew you when you were pregnant, or who remind you of your child.

• If you experience extreme emotions over a prolonged period and the emotions keep you from fully functioning. Extremes can include guilt, depression, low self-worth or extremely high spirits.

Suicidal plans. Have you had suicidal thoughts? Many parents have had fleeting thoughts about suicide. The thought has come and gone, perhaps even more than a few times. But dwelling on these thoughts, writing out a plan of action or repeatedly fantasizing about your death, is a red flag. If you are having these thoughts, drop this book and get the professional help you need. If you don't have insurance, Pastors and clergy usually offer free counseling services. The armed forces also offers free behavioral health services through the hospital on the installation, for those qualified to use military benefits. Do not attempt to work through suicidal feelings on your own.

Use of illegal drugs or overuse of alcohol and prescription drugs. Try an unmedicated approach to grief. When we mention "self-medicated" we're talking about uncontrolled use of prescription drugs, illegal drugs or alcohol to numb the pain of grief. I had a C-section and remember using pain pills to sleep through the first three days after our second trimester loss. I didn't want to work through the pain and no one had the heart to force me. After those three days, I chose to confront my anguish. When the medication wears off, you will still be faced with the pain.

THE FIRST YEAR AND BEYOND:
The first anniversary of your loss, due date and other painful occasions.
The one year mark is undeniably a very large, hard obstacle and there is no getting around it. Most moms remember feeling anger, depression and sadness. Many cried and felt emptiness. Most parents agree that memorializing your baby is important. My husband and I talked and cried for our child all day. One mother needed serious distractions, so she went to the spa, planned a vacation and spent money on other people's children. Another parent released balloons; another lit a candle and reflected on her babies' lives with thanks and love mixed with grief. Visit some of the Web sites in the *Additional Reading* section for other suggestions.

Write about your baby's life. Writing is therapeutic. Write from the heart and include how you felt when you found out you were pregnant. Document other people's reactions to your hopes and dreams for your baby. Share your love. Allow yourself to fully feel. Don't stop writing even if your heart hurts, hand trembles and your tears blur the pages.

Reach out to other hurting parents. Turn your hurt out, don't keep it in! Grief will isolate you, if you let it. Just like you, other grieving parents need someone to hear about their pain as part of the healing process.

Continue to celebrate your life. Make a choice to enjoy your time on this earth. Any child would want that for their parents.

Find meaning in life. Sometimes staying busy through your usual job no longer cuts it. Aggressively seek out the meaning for your life. Try not to focus on *"what* *happened?"* but on *"who am I now?"* Neither of these answers comes easily, but asking what happened? may leave you stranded in the past while who am I now? speaks to your future.

SOME FRIENDLY ADVICE:
If you are a friend ... here's how you can help
Understand that every parent won't want to talk about their internal pain.
You can let your grieving friend know you're there for them without bringing up the subject of their stolen angel.

Just be there, listen and accept. Do not offer false hope or assurances like "You'll bounce right back from this" or "I know how you feel" or "Everything will be fine." One day everything will be fine, but today the grieving parent just needs to know that you will listen. It is okay to admit that you don't understand what they are going through, but you can see that it is painful and difficult. Watching your friend struggle may bring up memories you have of a previous family member or friend's death. Perhaps you also mourn the loss of the baby who has died. Don't use your "support network" time to work through your grief. This may place the mourner in the unfortunate position of trying to comfort you!

Encourage. Strongly urge your grief-filled friend to leave the house. Sometimes, the home can be like a tomb – it feels almost impossible to get out!

Realize if you haven't lost a baby, you don't understand. Do not talk about the loss of your pet, your grandmother's death, or any death that is not the loss of a child. Don't say "I know how you feel" because each person grieves differently. If you have also lost a child, use your loss as a way to mention similarities. Any feedback, insight or personal stories have so much more meaning when the bereaved knows you've gone through a similar loss.

Don't say anything. Sometimes the best thing you can do is to sit quietly.

Know the symptoms of depression. After the birth of a baby, women are susceptible to depression, but the "baby blues" usually pass after a period of time. Full blown depression requires immediate intervention, but with emotional support and treatment from a caring professional, recovery is within reach. If you see several of the symptoms listed below, gently but persistently encourage professional help. The National Institute of Mental Health describes depression as:

- Persistent sad, anxious, or "empty" mood
- Feelings of hopelessness, pessimism
- Feelings of guilt, worthlessness, helplessness
- Loss of interest or pleasure in hobbies and activities that were once enjoyed, including sex
- Decreased energy, fatigue, being "slowed down"
- Difficulty concentrating, remembering, making decisions
- Insomnia, early-morning awakening, or oversleeping
- Appetite and/or weight loss or overeating and weight gain
- Thoughts of death or suicide; suicide attempts
- Restlessness, irritability
- Persistent physical symptoms that do not respond to treatment, such as headaches, digestive disorders, and chronic pain

There are many types and degrees of depression, it is best to leave its diagnosis to the professionals.

CHILDREN AND GRIEF: Talking about your loss

Communication do's and don'ts. Here is a list of do's and don'ts from www.bereavedparents.com for communicating with your child about the families' loss.

Do's

- Do be open with your own emotions – "I'm very sad."
- Do be explicit about why you feel as you do – "Your baby brother died."
- Do be specific about why the death occurred – "Your baby sister died because she was born too soon."
- Do be short on word answers and long on hugs of reassurance.
- Do include children of all ages in the family's rituals of leave-taking.

Don'ts

- Don't talk too much. Answer only those questions a child asks, or special concerns you think they may have.

- Don't try to do your children's mourning for them. You won't succeed.
- Don't pass off the child's fears as inappropriate. They are real.
- Don't pretend that nothing significant has happened.
- Don't try to stop the mourning process.
- Don't provide junk food or drink for your children; limit treats to special occasions.

Signs of grief in children. Expressing a wide range of emotions is healthy. Children do grieve, but differently from adults. A child experiences more acute ups and downs, so respect your child's emotions, but help them find limits to the extreme ranges of emotions. One minute they may laugh, but the next they may cry. Children may become depressed, accident prone or express feelings in a violent manner at home or at school. Show surviving children a lot of affection and talk openly about how you feel. Help them identify their own feelings, as well. An older child may have a never-ending stream of questions about what happened. Try to be patient when answering these questions; they may be trying to express a different thought although the same words are being used. Other tips from www.bereavedparents.com:

- Ensure you have a good support network so that when grief prevents you from responding to your child's needs, extended family or a professional can help.
- Provide opportunities for the entire family to share feelings and memories about your baby.
- If you or your surviving children are feeling overwhelmed, don't be afraid to reach out to a professional grief counselor.
- * For more grief survival tips, visit www.infantloss.blogspot.com

ADDITIONAL READING

BOOKS

Facing the Ultimate Loss; Coping with the Death of a Child by Robert J. Marx and Susan Wengerhoff Davidson

Grief Steps: 10 Steps to Regroup, Rebuild and Renew after any Life Loss by Brook Noel

When There Are No Words: Finding Your Way to Cope With Loss and Grief by Charlie Walton

When a Baby Dies: A Handbook for Healing and Helping by Rana K. Limbo & Sara Rich Wheeler

Surviving Holidays, Birthdays & Anniversaries: A Guide for Grieving During Special Occasions by Brook Noel

The SIDS Survival Guide: Information and Comfort for Grieving Family & Friends & Professionals Who Seek to Help Them by Joani Nelson Horchler & Robin Rice Morris

A Time to Grieve: Meditations for Healing After the Death of a Loved One by Carol Staudacher

Free To Grieve: Healing and Encouragement for Those Who Have Suffered Miscarriage and Stillbirth by Maureen Rank

How Can I Help?: How to Support Someone Who is Grieving by June Cerza Kolf

How Do We Tell the Children? A Step-By-Step Guide for Helping Children Two to Teen Cope When Someone Dies, 3rd Edition by Dan

Schaefer, Ph.D., & Christine Lyons

ONLINE HELP

A Place to Remember
www.aplacetoremember.com
Message boards for parents experiencing a variety of concerns including NICU loss, problem pregnancy, miscarriage, termination, stillbirth and infant death. I especially like the catalog of 120 books and pamphlets. Click "Grief" then "Product Mall."

AMEND
(Aiding Mothers and Fathers Experiencing Neonatal Death)
www.amendgroup.com
Free one-on-one counseling services by parents who have experienced the loss through miscarriage, stillbirth, or neonatal death. Counselors are not psychologists, but have been trained by professionals. Call Maureen Connelly, 24-hours a day at 314-487-7582.

Bereaved Parents
www.bereavedparents.com
Offers useful information and support to anyone who has lost a child. I especially like the "How to Respond" section. With creative ways other parents have responded to others' questions.

Bereavement Services Support and Education
www.bereavement.net
Visit this site for a list of books suitable for children and teens dealing with the loss of their sibling. At the top of their home page, click on "Reading."

Beyond Indigo
www.beyondindigo.com

Participate in message boards, create a memorial, read articles and more.

Centering Corporation
www.centering.org

This non-profit organization sells more than 300 resources for the bereaved. Paid membership allows access to a quarterly magazine and more. Call toll-free 866-218-0101 for more information or to request a catalog.

Compassionate Friends
www.compassionatefriends.org

A free, national nonprofit, self-help support organization offering friendship, understanding, and hope to families grieving the death of a child of any age. Call toll-free 877-969-0010 for a referral to a local chapter or to receive grief-related information.

Good Grief Resources
www.goodgriefresources.com

Offers a variety of sources for the bereaved including memorial products, poems, articles, books, support groups, and an online store.

Hannah's Prayer
www.hannah.org

An online community for married, Christian women who are seeking God to help with infertility, pregnancy loss, infant death and failed adoption. They offer more than 70 support groups and a list of other Christian loss organizations.

Hygeia Foundation
www.hygeia.org

Builds awareness and recovery when children die. Provides burial assistance to low-income families, information about healthcare and access to more than 27,000 members in its international community. Call toll-free 1-800-893-9198

Infant Loss Support
www.infantloss.blogspot.com

This is my personal blog (Sharee's). I offer more tried and true healing tips, insight, Web sights of interest and more. It's an easy way to talk to someone who knows their way around (and out) of a world weighted by grief.

Memory-Of.com
www.memory-of.com

Create a memorial Web site in a community committed to keeping your loved one's memory alive. Also, participate in message boards.

M.I.S.S. (Mothers in Sympathy & Support)
www.missfoundation.org

Provides crisis support and long-term help for the entire family after the death of an infant or young child. Offers online and local support groups, a therapist finder, workshops, stories, information about funerals, a corner for professionals, and more.

PASS Awareness – Post Abortion Stress Syndrome
http://afterabortion.com

A place of healing and support free from the pro-life, pro-choice debate. Message boards, chat, e-mail lists, resources for fathers, and more.

National SIDS/Infant Death Resource Center
www.sidscenter.org

Provides information services and assistance on Sudden Infant Death Syndrome (SIDS) and related topics.

Parents of Murdered Children, Inc.
www.pomc.com

Helps parents and other survivors reconstruct a "new life" and to promote a healthy resolution. It helps survivors deal with their acute

grief and the criminal justice system, as well. Call toll-free 888 818-
POMC

SHARE – Pregnancy & Infant Loss Support
www.nationalshareoffice.com

Serves those who are touched by the tragic death of a baby through miscarriage, stillbirth, or newborn death. Provides live chat, resources, online shopping and more. Call the National Share Office, toll-free at 800-821-6819.

S.P.A.L.S. (Subsequent Pregnancy after a Loss Support)
www.spals.com

SPALS is a safe haven for bereaved parents who are considering another pregnancy. Includes an active support network of over 400 members.

MILITARY RESOURCES

ARMY
Army Community Service

NAVY & MARINES
Fleet and Family Support Center

AIR FORCE
Airmen and Family Readiness Center

Stolen Angels

Quick Order Form

Telephone Orders: Call 610-906-3386

E-mail orders: orders@dynastybookpublishers.com

Mailed orders: Dynasty Publishers, LLC
ATTN Sales
P.O. Box 30774,
Clarksville, TN 37040

Please send: *Stolen Angels: 25 Stories of Hope after Pregnancy or Infant Loss.* I understand that I may return this book for a refund within 90 days of purchase. Your satisfaction with this product is our priority.

Please send FREE information about:

Other Products   Speaking/Seminars   Mailing Lists

Pregnancy and Infant Loss   Miscarriage Prevention

Pregnancy after Loss

Name: _____

Address: _____

City: _____State: _____Zip: _____

Telephone: _____

E-mail: _____

Price per book: $15.95
Sales Tax for Tennessee addresses only: $1.52 per book
Shipping rate: $4 for the first book and $1 for each additional book.

Total dollar amount enclosed or charged: _____

Circle Payment Type: Check   Visa   MasterCard

Card Number: _____

Expiration date: _____

Name on Card: _____

Stolen Angels

Quick Order Form

Telephone Orders: Call 610-906-3386

E-mail orders: orders@dynastybookpublishers.com

Mailed orders: Dynasty Publishers, LLC
ATTN Sales
P.O. Box 30774,
Clarksville, TN 37040

Please send: *Stolen Angels: 25 Stories of Hope after Pregnancy or Infant Loss.* I understand that I may return this book for a refund within 90 days of purchase. Your satisfaction with this product is our priority.

Please send FREE information about:

Other Products   Speaking/Seminars   Mailing Lists

Pregnancy and Infant Loss   Miscarriage Prevention

Pregnancy after Loss

Name: _____

Address: _____

City: _____ **State:** _____ **Zip:** _____

Telephone: _____

E-mail: _____

Price per book: $15.95
Sales Tax for Tennessee addresses only: $1.52 per book
Shipping rate: $4 for the first book and $1 for each additional book.

Total dollar amount enclosed or charged: _____

Circle Payment Type: Check   Visa   MasterCard

Card Number: _____

Expiration date: _____

Name on Card: _____

Quick Order Form

Telephone Orders: Call 610-906-3386

E-mail orders: orders@dynastybookpublishers.com

Mailed orders: Dynasty Publishers, LLC
ATTN Sales
P.O. Box 30774,
Clarksville, TN 37040

Please send: *Stolen Angels: 25 Stories of Hope after Pregnancy or Infant Loss.* I understand that I may return this book for a refund within 90 days of purchase. Your satisfaction with this product is our priority.

Please send FREE information about:

Other Products   Speaking/Seminars   Mailing Lists

Pregnancy and Infant Loss   Miscarriage Prevention

Pregnancy after Loss

Name: _____

Address: _____

City: _____State: _____Zip: _____

Telephone: _____

E-mail: _____

Price per book: $15.95
Sales Tax for Tennessee addresses only: $1.52 per book
Shipping rate: $4 for the first book and $1 for each additional book.

Total dollar amount enclosed or charged: _____

Circle Payment Type: Check   Visa   MasterCard

Card Number: _____

Expiration date: _____

Name on Card: _____

Stolen Angels

Quick Order Form

Telephone Orders: Call 610-906-3386

E-mail orders: orders@dynastybookpublishers.com

Mailed orders: Dynasty Publishers, LLC
ATTN Sales
P.O. Box 30774,
Clarksville, TN 37040

Please send: *Stolen Angels: 25 Stories of Hope after Pregnancy or Infant Loss.* I understand that I may return this book for a refund within 90 days of purchase. Your satisfaction with this product is our priority.

Please send FREE information about:

Other Products   Speaking/Seminars   Mailing Lists

Pregnancy and Infant Loss   Miscarriage Prevention

Pregnancy after Loss

Name: _____

Address: _____

City: _____State: _____Zip: _____

Telephone: _____

E-mail: _____

Price per book: $15.95
Sales Tax for Tennessee addresses only: $1.52 per book
Shipping rate: $4 for the first book and $1 for each additional book.

Total dollar amount enclosed or charged: _____

Circle Payment Type: Check   Visa   MasterCard

Card Number: _____

Expiration date: _____

Name on Card: _____